Illustrated
SCIENCE and
TECHNOLOGY
DICTIONARY

Illustrated
SCIENCE and
TECHNOLOGY
DICTIONARY

An Essential Student Resource

Cheryl Jakab

David Keystone

Good Year Books

Parsippany, New Jersey

Good Year Books
are available for most basic curriculum subjects plus many enrichment areas. For more
Good Year Books, contact your local bookseller or educational dealer. For a complete
catalog with information about other Good Year Books, please write:

Good Year Books
An imprint of Pearson Learning
299 Jefferson Road, P.O. Box 480
Parsippany, NJ 07054-0480

www.pearsonlearning.com

1-800-321-3106

Cover Design: Elaine Lopez
Interior Illustrations: Wendy Gorton, John Ward, and Scott Quick
Design Manager: M. Jane Heelan
Editorial Manager: Constance Shrier
Executive Editor: Judith Adams
Production/Manufacturing Director: Janet Yearian
Production/Manufacturing Manager: Karen Edmonds
Production/Manufacturing Coordinator: Julie Ryan

ISBN 0-673-59960-4

7 8 - SCG - 08 07 06

Contents

Introduction

Children are inherently curious. They constantly ask questions about their world, including its scientific and technological features. Indeed, the technological world is becoming more and more complex because of our changing scientific understandings. To function effectively, we all need an awareness of science and technology, and this includes a wide vocabulary of terms to be used accurately.

In science and technology teaching and learning, words and their meanings are becoming more valued as we realize just how important terms are in the development of ideas. Ideas are expressed through words—words for which we need shared meanings.

This dictionary is designed to provide students with scientifically accurate meanings of the most commonly used terms in the science and technology classroom. The definitions are expressed in simple language that all students should be able to understand. The dictionary makes the definitions clear, while maintaining precision and accuracy. Illustrations and examples are used throughout to support and expand the written definitions.

Although this book was designed primarily to help students with their scientific and technological literacy, teachers and parents will also find its simple definitions of great assistance to their own understanding.

Cheryl Jakab and David Keystone

abdomen

A part of an animal's body. In humans and other vertebrates, between the shoulder and the hip. It contains the stomach and other organs. It is found in the rear section of a spider or insect.

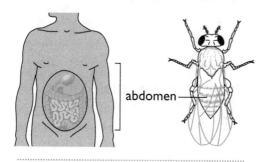

abdomen

abrasive

A gritty substance used for rubbing or grinding.

absorb

To soak up. For example, a sponge absorbs liquid.

acid

Characteristic of chemicals containing hydrogen. Weak acids have a sour taste. Strong acids produce a burning sensation if they make contact with the skin. Acids dissolve or corrode many metals and turn blue litmus paper red.

Common Household Acids

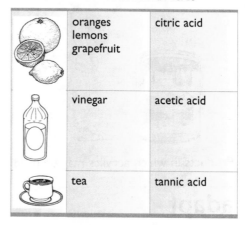

	oranges lemons grapefruit	citric acid
	vinegar	acetic acid
	tea	tannic acid

See *pH*.

acoustics

(i) The study of sound and sound waves.
(ii) Properties of a building relating to how well sounds such as speech and music may be heard clearly.

See *sound*.

acrylic

Acrylic compounds are manufactured as plastics, fibers, or resins. Lucite® and Plexiglas® are examples of common acrylics. Acrylic compounds soften when heated and harden when cooled.

Products in which acrylics may be used

adapt

To change in order to better fit new conditions or circumstances. For example, beaks of birds are adapted to suit their diet.

The spoonbill's wide beak is adapted for catching fish and aquatic insects.

aerodynamics

(i) The study of the forces acting on an object as it moves through air or some other gas.
(ii) Forces that act on airplanes and any other object moving through the air.

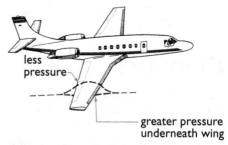

less pressure

greater pressure underneath wing

Drag and lift are aerodynamic forces. Aircraft are streamlined to reduce drag and increase lift.

See *drag*.

agate

Semiprecious hard stone. Often marked with stripes, bands, or swirls of color.

See *gemstone, rock*.

air

Invisible gases that surround the earth. A mixture of nitrogen, oxygen, and small amounts of other gases.

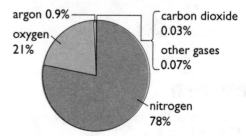

argon 0.9%

oxygen 21%

carbon dioxide 0.03%

other gases 0.07%

nitrogen 78%

Mixture of gases in air

airplane

A machine-driven aircraft capable of flight. Heavier than air.

air pressure

Pressure caused by the movement of molecules in air. Air that is forced into a given space, such as in a tire, balloon, or basketball, increases the pressure inside the space.

See *molecule*.

albumen

Part of the egg of a bird and some reptiles; referred to as the egg white. It is watery and lies between the shell and the yolk.

See *yolk*.

algae

(plural; singular: alga)

Moisture-loving plants that live in water. They make their own food using light energy. Algae may be green, brown, or red.

See *seaweed*.

alimentary canal

The passage inside an animal's body leading from the mouth to the anus. It digests and absorbs food and removes waste from the body.

See *digestive system*.

alkaline

Describing the characteristic of chemicals that form salts when combined with acids. Weak alkalis are soapy to touch. Strong alkalis are caustic (or corrosive). Also referred to as a base substance.

Common Household Alkalis

	"cleaning" ammonia	ammonium hydroxide
	baking soda	sodium bicarbonate
	lye	sodium hydroxide

See *ph*.

allergy

A major reaction to a substance to which the body has become sensitive. Asthma, hay fever, hives, and eczema are examples of allergic reactions.

aluminum

A silvery grey, lightweight metal. It is used to make drink cans, aircraft, and cooking utensils. It can be rolled out thinly to make foil.

See *metal*.

amber

Hard yellow-brown fossil resin produced by certain trees millions of years ago. It can contain preserved insects, flowers, or leaves that were trapped by the sticky surface. Occurs throughout the world in various rocks. Acquires an electrical charge when rubbed. Also used for making jewelry and ornaments.

amethyst

Violet- or purple-colored precious stone. A variety of quartz.

See *gemstone, quartz*.

amphibian

An animal that lives both on land and in water, for example, a frog, toad, newt, and salamander. Its skin is moist and slimy.

anatomy

(i) The structure of the bodies of plants or animals.
(ii) The study of the structure of the bodies of plants or animals.

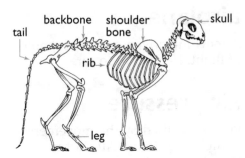

(a) The structure of a cat's skeleton

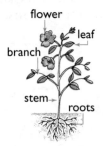

(b) The structure of a plant

anemometer

An instrument for measuring the speed of wind and, sometimes, its direction.

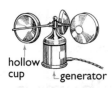

animal

A living thing that feeds on other living things. Most animals are able to move about. Commonly divided into invertebrate (an animal without a backbone) and vertebrate (an animal with a backbone).

Examples of vertebrate animals

Examples of invertebrate animals

See *kingdom*.

ant

An insect that lives in a community known as a colony. It has a narrow waist between its thorax and abdomen.

See *abdomen, insect, thorax.*

antenna

(i) The sense organ or feeler found in pairs on the heads of insects, crabs, and other invertebrates.
(ii) Wire or aerial used to send or receive signals, as in a television or radio antenna.

antibiotic

A drug used to kill bacteria and fungi that cause or carry disease. Produced by living organisms such as fungi. The first antibiotic used was penicillin.

antiseptic

A chemical used on a surface, such as the skin, to kill tiny organisms that could produce infection.

aorta

The major artery that carries blood away from the left side of the heart to the rest of the body.

See *artery, circulatory system, heart.*

apparatus

A collection of machines and tools especially used to perform scientific experiments.

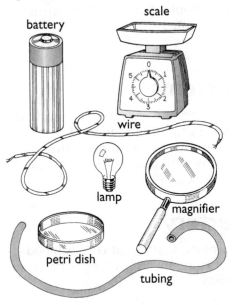

arachnid

An arthropod with eight legs and two major body parts, for example, spiders, scorpions.

See *arthropod, spider.*

arch

A curved structure that helps to support. It may form an entrance or doorway.

argon

A colorless, odorless, nonreactive gas. Called an inert gas. Used in electric light tubes. Argon makes up about 1 percent of the earth's atmosphere.

See *air, gas.*

arsenic

An element occurring naturally in the earth and sea in very small amounts. In larger quantities it is a powerful poison. Has been used as a pest killer.

artery

A blood vessel that carries blood from the heart to other parts of the body.

See *circulatory system, vein.*

arthropod

An invertebrate animal. It has pairs of jointed limbs and a segmented body. The hard outer casing is shed in order for the animal to grow. Includes insects, spiders, crabs, millipedes, and shrimp.

See *animal.*

asteroid

Minor planets of rock and iron. Most have orbits that lie between the orbits of Mars and Jupiter. Ceres is the largest-known asteroid. There may be as many as 100,000 asteroids in the solar system.

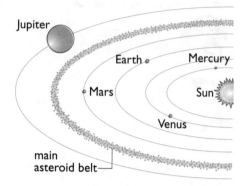

Main asteroid belt in the solar system

astronaut

A person especially trained to travel and work in space.

astronomy

The study of the sun, moon, stars, planets, and other objects in space.

atmosphere

Mixture of gases that surround the earth, appearing in set layers.

Layers of the Earth's Atmosphere

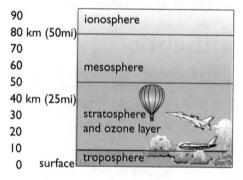

atom

Tiny particles that make up matter. Carbon is made of carbon atoms; oxygen of oxygen atoms. Atoms are the smallest particles of chemical elements. They consist of a small nucleus of protons and neutrons surrounded by moving electrons.

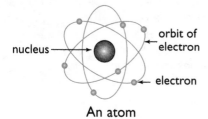

An atom

See *electron, element, nucleus, proton.*

attract

To draw closer or pull something, as steel is pulled to a magnet.

See *magnet.*

axle

A rod or bar on which a wheel rotates.

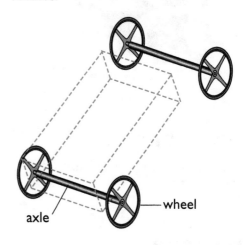

backbone

The column of bones forming the spine.

See *vertebra*.

bacteria

(plural; singular: bacterium)

Microscopic organisms without a nucleus. They are grouped, according to their shape, into spheres, rods, or spirals.

spheres   rods   spirals

Three shapes of bacteria

bacteriology

The study of bacteria.

See *bacteria*.

balance

(i) A device for measuring weight or mass.
(ii) The ability to stand upright or in equilibrium, as in "I can balance on my skates."

bark

The woody outer covering of tree trunks and branches.

See *tree*.

barometer

An instrument that measures the pressure of the atmosphere. It is used to show changes in weather conditions.

See *atmosphere*.

basalt

The most common volcanic rock. It is formed when lava cools on the Earth's surface

See *volcanic rock*.

base

A term used to describe alkaline substances.

See *alkaline*.

battery

A device made by joining up electric cells to provide electricity. Examples of common batteries are dry batteries (used in most household items), acid batteries (such as a car battery), and lithium batteries (used to power some heart pacemakers and computers).

See *electricity*.

Beaufort wind scale

A scale from 0–12 that is used to measure wind strength. Devised by Francis Beaufort in 1806. It is based on observed effects in the environment.

Number	Description	Features	Speed km/h
0	calm	smoke rises vertically; water smooth	less than 1
1	light air	smoke shows wind direction; water ruffles	1–5
2	slight breeze	leaves rustle; wind felt on face	6–11
3	gentle breeze	loose paper blows around	12–19
4	moderate breeze	branches sway	20–28
5	fresh breeze	small trees sway, leaves blown off	29–38
6	strong breeze	whistling in telephone wires; sea spray from waves	39–49
7	moderate gale	large trees sway	50–61
8	fresh gale	twigs break from trees	62–74
9	strong gale	branches break from trees	75–88
10	whole gale	trees uprooted; weak buildings collapse	89–102
11	storm	widespread damage	103–117
12	hurricane	widespread structural damage	118 and over

beetle

A type of insect with front wings forming a hard wing covering, for example, a ladybug beetle.

See *insect*.

big bang

The theory that the universe began about 15 billion years ago from the explosion of a single point. According to this theory, matter spreading outward from that explosion formed the galaxies, stars, and planets that fill the universe today.

See *theory*.

binoculars

An instrument with a pair of lenses that make distant objects appear larger and closer.

An adjusting ring moves the eyepieces in and out of the tube to adjust the focus.

eyepiece

objective lens

biodegradable

Able to be broken down by microscopic organisms such as bacteria and fungi.

See *decomposer*.

biology

The study of the structure, function, and development of living things.

See *living thing*.

biome

A large region that has a particular climate and distinct plant and animal life, for example, a desert. Biomes may be on land or in the water. On land, factors such as rainfall, elevation, temperature, and soil type help to determine the organisms that make up the biome.

See *biosphere, community, ecosystem, population*.

biosphere

The regions of earth where life exists. The biosphere includes some of the earth's surface (lithosphere), its waters (hydrosphere), and the lower atmosphere.

See *biome, community, ecosystem, population.*

bird

An animal with a backbone and feathers. Birds are warm-blooded.

See *warm-blooded.*

birth

The coming into the world of a new baby animal; the act of being born.

See *life cycle.*

bit

(short for "binary digit")
A single basic unit of information, used in connection with computers. Eight bits make a unit called a byte.

See *computer.*

black hole

A relatively small object in space that has a mass so large that its gravity prevents light from escaping. Such objects appear black to observers on Earth.

blizzard

Winter storms with very low temperatures, high winds, and snow. In order for a snowstorm to be called a blizzard, wind speed must be at least 35 miles per hour, and the temperature must be 20 degrees F or lower.

blood

Fluid that circulates through the body and which carries oxygen and nutrients and removes wastes. Blood is made up mainly of blood cells and water.

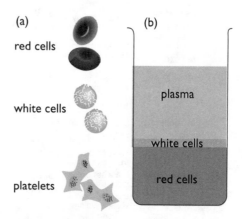

(a)
red cells

white cells

platelets

(b)
plasma

white cells

red cells

(a) Blood cells
(b) Blood allowed to stand separates into layers.

blossom

A flower or mass of flowers; the state of flowering.

boil

To react to heat; to change from a liquid to a gas when heated. Liquid water turns into steam, a gas, when heated.

boiling point

The temperature at which a liquid boils. Water boils at 100 degrees Celsius or 212 degrees Fahrenheit.

See *boil, Celsius scale, Fahrenheit scale.*

bone

Hard tissue that makes up the skeletons of most vertebrates.

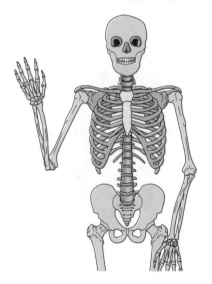

The human skeleton is made up of many bones.

botany

The study of plants.

See *plant.*

bowel

A long tubelike organ in the body. Part of the digestive system. It is also known as the large intestine. Water is absorbed through the bowel.

See *digestive system, large intestine.*

brain

The soft tissue inside the skull. The brain is the control center of the body.

See *nervous system.*

breathing

The process of taking in air through the nose and mouth into the lungs and reversing the process to let out air.

See *respiratory system.*

bridge

(i) A structure built over a depression to allow traffic to pass across. Bridges may be built over water, valleys, or roads.
(ii) The upper part of the nose.

See *nose.*

bronze

A shiny reddish metal made by combining copper and tin.

See *metal.*

bulb

(i) light bulb: A shaped glass that contains an electric-light filament.

(ii) plant bulb: The swollen underground part of certain plants, such as onions and daffodils.

buoyancy

The tendency to float or rise up on water.

butterfly

A type of insect with four opaque scaly wings, often brightly colored. Most butterflies fly by day. They usually have antennae that are shaped like clubs.

See *antenna, insect.*

buttress

A structure built on the outside of a wall to help support it.

cactus

A plant that grows in very dry areas; has a fleshy stem that retains moisture. Cactus plants often have prickly spines and bear colored flowers. Examples are the saguaro cactus and the prickly pear cactus.

See *plant.*

calcium

(i)   A soft, silvery metal.
(ii) A substance that is found in bone and teeth.

See *metal.*

camouflage

Commonly used to describe the way in which a creature blends with its surroundings using color, patterns, or shape.

A stick insect on a plant

carbohydrate

One of a group of chemicals including sugars and starches. Present in all living things. Bananas, potatoes, cereal, pasta, and bread are examples of foods rich in carbohydrates.

carbon

A nonmetal. It occurs in many forms, including coal and diamond. Carbon can form many different compounds. Carbon compounds are the basis of living tissue.

carbon dioxide

A colorless, odorless gas formed by burning carbon. Animals breathe out carbon dioxide. Plants use carbon dioxide in making food.

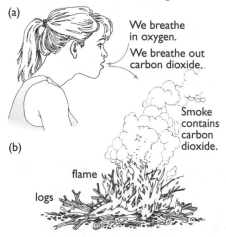

(a)

We breathe in oxygen.
We breathe out carbon dioxide.

Smoke contains carbon dioxide.

(b)

flame

logs

carnivore

An animal, for example, a cat, an eagle, a shark, and a meat-eating human, that feeds on the flesh of other animals.

cartilage

Gristle. Elastic and flexible tissue that forms part of a skeleton. In humans it is found between joints, in the top of the ear, and at the end of the nose. Some fish, such as sharks and rays, have skeletons of cartilage.

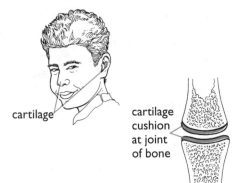

cartilage

cartilage cushion at joint of bone

See *joint*.

caterpillar

The grub or larva stage of a butterfly or moth. The grub hatches from the egg.

See *larva*.

CD

(short for "compact disk")

A disk that stores information. It is used in a compact disk player or computer. It reproduces music, video, graphics, or text.

cell

Microscopic structure of living things. An organism can be one-celled, as is an amoeba, or can be made up of many kinds of cells, such as blood, muscle, and nerve.

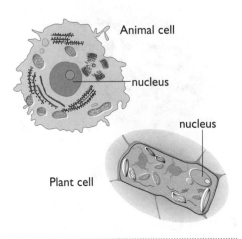

Animal cell

nucleus

nucleus

Plant cell

Celsius scale

A scale for measuring temperature. The symbol is C.

See *Fahrenheit scale, thermometer.*

chemical

Any substance related to chemistry.

See *chemistry.*

chemical reaction

When two or more substances combine to produce new substances.

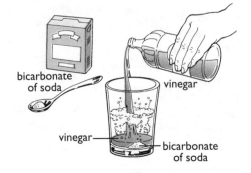

bicarbonate of soda

vinegar

vinegar

bicarbonate of soda

Adding vinegar to bicarbonate of soda sets off a chemical reaction.

chemistry

The study of the structure of chemicals and the ways chemicals are combined to make new chemicals.

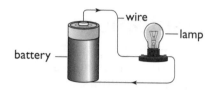

Electric circuit

See *electricity*.

chlorophyll

The pigment that gives the green color to parts of plants, such as that in the stems and the leaves. It traps and absorbs the energy from sunlight that plants use to make food.

chromosome

Small, threadlike bodies that can be seen in the nucleus of a cell when it divides. Chromosomes direct the activities of the cell. They are composed of many genes that carry hereditary information. The number of chromosomes in a cell is a characteristic of each species. Humans, for example, have 23 pairs of chromosomes.

circuit

A path over which electric current flows or is intended to flow. A simple electric circuit might have a battery, two wires (one end of each attached to each terminal of the battery), and a small lamp to which the free ends of the wires are attached.

circulatory system

(i) Parts of a plant that work together to make sap flow.
(ii) Parts of the body of an animal that work together to make the blood flow. Blood supplies oxygen and nutrients and removes wastes from parts of the body.

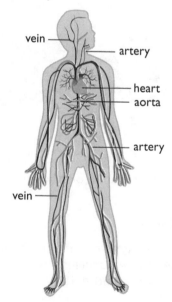

Veins transport blood to the heart. Arteries transport blood away from the heart.

classification

When similar things are sorted into groups, such as reptiles, mammals, and plants.

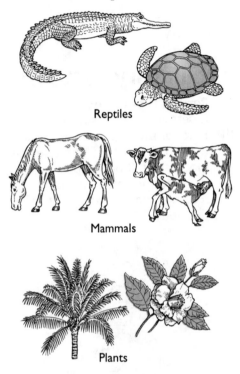

Reptiles

Mammals

Plants

A classification of living things

clay

Stiff, thick type of earth material made of fine particles. Used to make bricks and pottery.

See *soil*.

climate

The weather conditions, including temperature, rainfall, humidity, and wind, that occur in a particular area or region.

See *weather*.

clouds

Groups of water droplets floating in the air above ground level. A cloud's appearance is affected by its height above the ground.

The Altitude of Some Types of Clouds

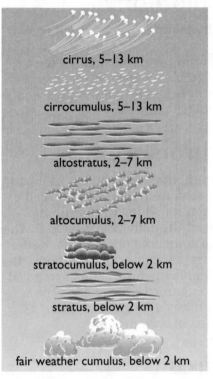

cirrus, 5–13 km

cirrocumulus, 5–13 km

altostratus, 2–7 km

altocumulus, 2–7 km

stratocumulus, below 2 km

stratus, below 2 km

fair weather cumulus, below 2 km

coal

Remains of dead plants, especially trees, which died many millions of years ago. Dark carbon substances formed under pressure. Coal is used as a fuel.

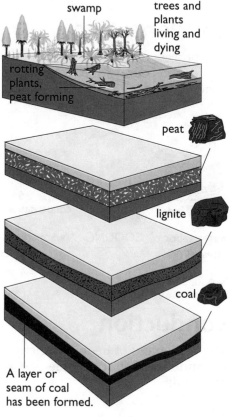

How coal forms

See *carbon, fossil fuel.*

cold-blooded

The term used to describe animals whose body temperature is not constant. It rises and falls to match the temperature of their surroundings. Cold-blooded animal groups include reptiles and fish.

See *warm-blooded.*

colony

A group of organisms of the same species that live and grow together. A colony of bacteria is the mass of offspring that arise from a single original cell.

color

(i) How light of a certain wavelength appears to the human eye.
(ii) How an object appears according to the type of light it reflects.

White light is made up of different colors. We detect the wavelength of light as color.

See *spectrum, wavelength.*

comet

Small icy body moving around the sun, having a bright head and very long tail. Comets are moving balls of gases, ice, and dust. Halley's comet is a bright comet and can be seen from Earth every 76 years.

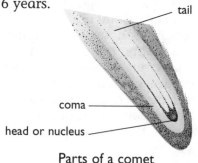

Parts of a comet

community

Groups of interacting plants and animals that live together in a given area. The plants, insects, birds, squirels, frogs, and other animals that live around your school make up a community.

See *ecosystem, population, succession.*

compass

An instrument that shows direction. The most commonly used compasses work by magnetism. Used in ships and airplanes.

compost

A mixture of rotting materials used as soil nutrient, for example, food and plant scraps in a compost bin. Heat helps the rotting process.

compound

Two or more elements joined together to form a new substance with properties that are very different from those of the original elements. Water is a compound made up of the elements hydrogen and oxygen. Compounds are formed when elements share electrons or when one element loses one or more electrons to the other element.

See *element, mixture.*

computer

An electronic device able to be programmed. Capable of accessing, storing, and manipulating data. It is used with a keyboard and monitor.

condensation

The process of change of a gas to a liquid. Fog is an example of condensation.

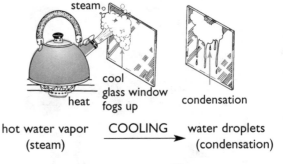

steam

cool glass window fogs up

heat

condensation

hot water vapor (steam)   COOLING ⟶   water droplets (condensation)

See *fog.*

conduction

The movement of heat, electricity, or sound through a suitable material.

(a)

The wire, battery, and lamp conduct electricity.

Metal conducts heat.

Warm air displaces cool air.

Cool air warms and rises.

Cool air sinks.

Cool air moves toward the heater.

The heater warms air in the room by convection.

Air conducts sound.

consumer

An organism that eats other organisms. Primary consumers feed on plants, for example, rabbits and kangaroos eat grass. Secondary consumers feed on primary consumers, for example, foxes eat rabbits.

convection

Movement of heat by circulating air or liquid.

copper

A reddish-brown-colored metal. Used to make electric wire.

See *metal*.

coral

(i) An invertebrate animal, related to jellyfish, with a hard outer covering.
(ii) Hard material creating sea reefs. Formed from skeletons of coral animals.

crab

A ten-legged crustacean with an abdomen and a short, broad body.

See *arthropod, crustacean*.

crustacean

One of many creatures belonging
to the class of arthropods that
includes crabs, lobsters, shrimps,
crayfish, prawns, krill. Crustaceans
have two major body parts, two
pairs of antennae,
and at least ten
major limbs.

See *arthropod, krill.*

crystal

Solid bodies with regular shapes
that include flat sides and angles.
The sides of crystals are called
faces.

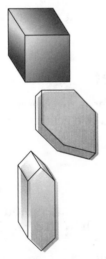

Forms of crystal systems

current

Stream or flow of air, water, heat,
or electricity in one direction, such
as the ocean currents that are
caused by wind patterns.

cycle

A recurring period of time in which
events repeat themselves in the
same order and at the same
intervals, such as the cycle of the
seasons on earth.

See *life cycle, water cycle.*

decomposer

An organism that breaks down or decomposes material from other living things such as plants or animal remains.

See *biodegradable.*

demonstrate

To show a process or phenomenon in a practical way, as in "I can demonstrate floating and sinking by placing a leaf and a rock in water."

density

The mass of a material in a given volume.

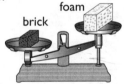

The brick is more dense than the foam.

desert

An area where the rainfall is too low to support most plant life.

diamond

The hardest crystal known, a form of carbon.

See *carbon, gemstone, Mohs scale.*

diaphragm

A thin layer of muscle in mammals between the chest cavity and the abdomen. It assists the lungs in the breathing process.

See *respiratory system.*

data

Facts or information collected through observations and tests. Now especially associated with computers.

Day	Size	Appearance
1		
5	1cm	
10	6cm	
15	15cm	

Data collected on the growth of a plant from a seed

day

The period of time in which the earth makes one turn on its axis; 24 hours, usually divided into two parts—daytime and nighttime.

deciduous

(i) Relating to trees and shrubs that shed their leaves each year, usually in autumn.
(ii) The first teeth in humans, which fall out to be replaced by adult teeth, are said to be deciduous teeth.

digestive system

The parts of an animal's body that carry out the breaking down of food. In complex animals, such as humans, this is made up of a tube with an opening at one end for food to go in and at the other end for the waste to leave the body. Parts include the mouth, stomach, intestines, and glands such as the liver and pancreas. In simple organisms, such as jellyfish, it can be a simple cavity with one opening.

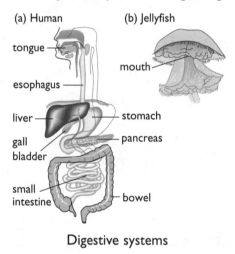

(a) Human   (b) Jellyfish

tongue
esophagus
liver
gall bladder
small intestine

mouth
stomach
pancreas
bowel

Digestive systems

dinosaur

Any of many species of extinct animals, related to birds and reptiles, that lived between 65 and 230 million years ago. Most were large, but many were as small as a chicken. The word "dinosaur" means terrible lizard.

Tyrannosaurus rex
Stegasaurus
Diplodocus
Coeluros

discover

To find out by looking or experimenting, as in "I am weighing these items to discover which one is the heaviest."

disease

A condition in the body of a living animal or plant that reduces its normal functioning. Infectious diseases are caused by bacteria, viruses, and other tiny organisms that spread among individuals. Hereditary diseases are caused by mistakes in the genetic code (DNA) that are passed from adults to their offspring.

See *immunize, infection, medicine, white blood cell.*

displace

To push aside. When a boat floats in water it displaces water equal to its weight.

See *float.*

dissolve

To absorb or melt into a liquid. For example, sugar dissolves when added to water.

DNA

A complex molecule that makes up the genes that form the chromosomes in the nucleus of living cells. DNA carries hereditary information in the form of a simple, four-symbol code found on the steps of its twisted, ladder-shaped molecules.

See *chromosome, gene.*

drag

The slowing effect that air, water, and other fluids can have on movement. It is caused by the friction between a moving object and the air or water through which it is moving.

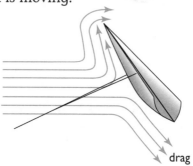

See *aerodynamics.*

ear

An organ that senses sound so an animal can hear. An ear is located on each side of the head.

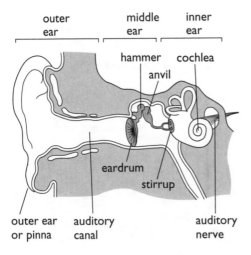

outer ear | middle ear | inner ear

hammer | cochlea
anvil

eardrum
stirrup

outer ear or pinna | auditory canal | auditory nerve

See *hearing, organ.*

earth

A term for soil, dust, dirt, or ground.

Earth

The planet we live on. Earth is the third planet from the sun.

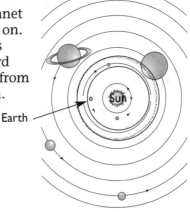

Earth

earthquake

A violent shaking of the earth's crust. Movement of the earth's surface caused by faults in the crust or volcanic activity.

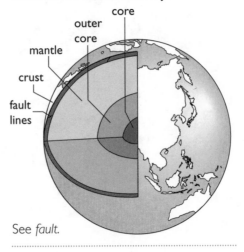

core
outer core
mantle
crust
fault lines

See *fault.*

earthworm

A soft-bodied invertebrate with damp skin and no legs. Earthworms live in the soil. They belong to a group of animals called Annelida.

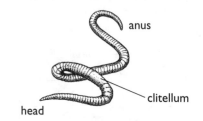

anus

clitellum

head

See *invertebrate*.

echo

The reflection of sound from a surface. For example, sound may echo in a gymnasium, cave, tunnel, pipe, or valley.

eclipse

When one astronomical body passes behind another body, becoming completely or partly hidden from view.

Earth

part shadow or penumbra

Moon

Sun

full shadow or umbra

Solar eclipse

See *lunar eclipse*, *solar eclipse*.

ecology

The study of the interactions of living things and their surroundings.

ecosystem

The system of relationships that exist in a community of living things in the place where they live, for example, in a pond, forest, or tree.

egg

(i) A round body that is produced by the female of a species and contains the beginnings of life.

(ii) The oval-shaped and often shell-covered form in which the young develop. A bird, reptile, insect, fish, or amphibian develops inside an egg.

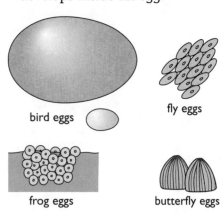

bird eggs

fly eggs

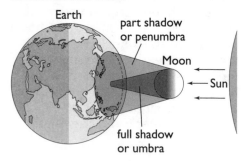

frog eggs

butterfly eggs

electricity

A form of energy produced by charged particles such as electrons. Electricity is changed into light, heat, magnetism, and mechanical motion. Electricity is used for lighting, heating, and making machines work.

Two sources of electricity are chemical (battery) and mechanical (generator).

See *battery, circuit, current, generator.*

electromagnet

A magnet made by passing electricity through a metal object such as a nail or bolt.

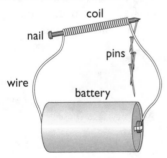

coil
nail
pins
wire
battery

The nail becomes an electromagnet when the current flows.

electromagnetic spectrum

A range of different types of electromagnetic waves and rays. It includes radio waves, television waves, microwaves, infrared rays, visible light rays, ultraviolet rays, and X-rays.

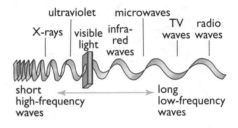

ultraviolet   microwaves
X-rays   visible   infra-   TV   radio
         light   red   waves waves
                   waves
short   long
high-frequency   low-frequency
waves   waves

See *light, wave.*

electron

A basic component of atoms with a negative electrical charge.

See *atom.*

element

A substance that cannot be broken down into a simpler substance by an ordinary physical or chemical process. An element is made up entirely of atoms that have the same number of protons. For example, hydrogen is an element because every hydrogen atom has one proton in its nucleus. Water is not an element because some of the atoms that join to form water have one proton (hydrogen) and others have eight protons (oxygen). Water is a compound.

See *atom, compound.*

el niño

Referring to warm currents of water in the Eastern Pacific Ocean that cause warming of the atmosphere and can lead to extreme weather conditions such as droughts.

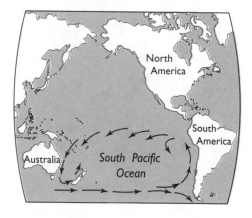

e-mail

Electronic mail. Information that is sent from one computer to another by way of the Internet.

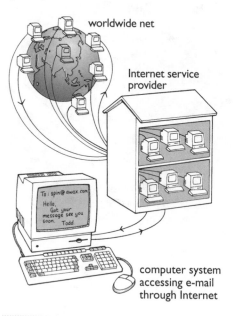

computer system accessing e-mail through Internet

enamel

A hard glossy coating that occurs naturally on teeth. Applied to the outer surfaces of pottery, metal, or painted surfaces as protection or decoration.

endangered

Referring to animal and plant species that are dangerously close to extinction, generally owing to destruction of their habitats. Examples of endangered animals are the Giant panda, rhinoceros, and tiger.

energy

The capacity to do work. Heat, light, sound, electricity, magnetism, and motion are forms of energy.

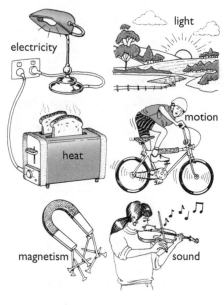

Examples of energy

See *electricity, heat, light, motion, sound.*

engine

A machine that uses energy to work. Commonly used to create movement, such as in a car, train, or airplane.

entomology

The study of insects.

See *insect, science.*

environment

The surroundings or conditions in which living things exist is called an environment.

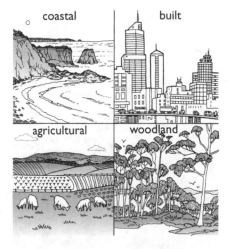

Examples of different environments

enzyme

One of many chemicals in the digestive system that break down food for use in the body. Enzymes break down food in the mouth, stomach, and small intestine.

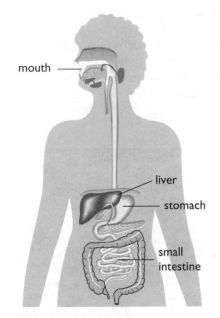

See *carbohydrate, fats, pancreas, stomach.*

equator

An imaginary line around the earth that divides it into two parts, the Northern Hemisphere and the Southern Hemisphere.

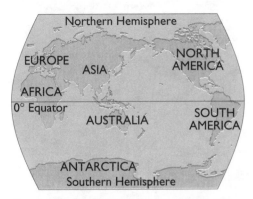

See *hemisphere, latitude.*

erosion

A process by which rock and soil are broken loose from the earth's surface. Rocks and soil are carried by water and wind.

(a) Cutting down and removing trees leads to erosion.

(b) The sea eroding a cliff

See *weathering*.

estimate

(i) To guess the value, size, or amount of something, as in "I estimate that the liquid will measure two quarts."
(ii) A guess of the value, size, or amount of something.

evaporation

The change of a liquid to a gas or vapor. Heating up a liquid such as water or milk causes it to evaporate into the air.

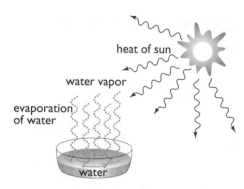

Evaporation of water caused by the heat of the sun

evergreen

Referring to a tree or shrub that has living leaves throughout the entire year. It sheds leaves from the past growing season only when new leaves have formed. Examples are palms, pine trees, and gums.

See *deciduous*.

evolution

The term used to refer to a gradual development over a long period of time. Using fossil evidence, change can be observed in the bodies of living things over millions of years.

Australopithecus (3 million years ago) Homo erectus (750,000 years ago) Homo sapiens (100,000 years ago)

Evolution of the human skull

excretory system

Parts of the body that produce and excrete urine. Organs include the kidneys, bladder, and urethra. The excretory system is involved in cleaning the blood and maintaining the proper balance between water and minerals in the blood stream.

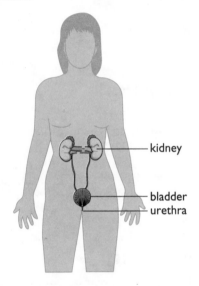

kidney

bladder
urethra

exoskeleton

A skeleton that lies outside the body tissues of an animal. Examples include the shells of mollusks, crustaceans, insects, and spiders. The exoskeleton is shed as the organism grows.

See *invertebrate*.

experiment

(i) To carry out a test to find out what will happen, as in "I will experiment to find out which powders dissolve in water."
(ii) A test to find out what will happen.

extinct

(i) Describes species of living things that have died out completely. Extinct animals include the dodo, Tasmanian tiger, passenger pigeon, and dinosaurs.
(ii) Describes a volcano that no longer erupts and is no longer active.

See *endangered*.

eye

The organ in animals for sensing light. The sense organ for seeing. Eyes are located on the face.

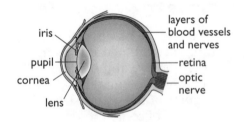

iris
pupil
cornea
lens
layers of blood vessels and nerves
retina
optic nerve

See *iris, lens, organ, pupil, retina*.

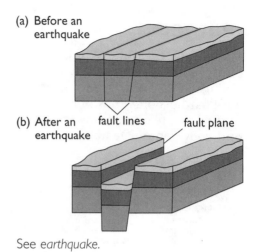

(a) Before an earthquake

(b) After an earthquake fault lines fault plane

Fahrenheit scale

A scale used to measure temperature. The symbol is F.

See *Celsius scale, thermometer.*

fats

One group of greasy, oily substances. Some fats are solid at room temperature. Most fats are produced in the body of animals but are also present in nuts and seeds, such as almonds, soybeans, corn, and cotton. Fats are an important part of the diet.

fault

A crack in the earth's crust caused by movement of rock layers. Movement along the fault line causes tremors and earthquakes.

See *earthquake.*

fauna

Referring to all the animal species living in a particular area, as in "the fauna of Asia."

See *flora.*

fax

The short version of the term *facsimile.* An exact copy of a document sent across telephone lines as digital information. A fax is made up of tiny dots.

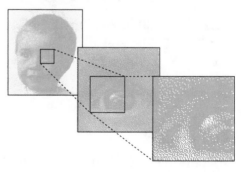

feather

Material on the outer skin layer of birds. Feathers keep birds warm and assist in flight. Types include quill feathers on wings and tails, fluffy down feathers for warmth, and body-contour feathers.

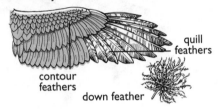

quill feathers

contour feathers

down feather

feces

Remains of food and other material passed out of the digestive tract.

See *digestive system, waste.*

femur

The upper leg bone in humans or the upper rear leg bone in four-legged animals.

See *skeleton.*

fern

One of more than 7,000 species of plants that reproduce by spores, not seeds. Fern leaves are called fronds.

See *frond, spore.*

fertilize

To join an egg and sperm to form a new life (at this early stage, called a zygote).

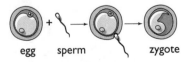

egg   sperm   zygote

fiber

A thin strand of material composed of threads. Fibers may be natural products such as wool, silk, and cotton, or man-made synthetics such as rayon and polyester.

fibula

One of the two bones in the lower leg in humans or one of the two lower rear leg bones in four-legged animals.

See *skeleton.*

filament

Fine wire in a light bulb that glows when electricity is passed through it.

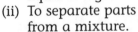

the metal wire filament

The filament is held up on a glass frame.

film

(i) Any thin layer of material, as in "a film of oil on water."
(ii) A roll of transparent material coated with a chemical that will react to light, for use in photography or movie making.

filter

(i) A device for separating a solid from a liquid or a gas.
(ii) To separate parts from a mixture.
(iii) A substance that allows only certain colors of light to pass through.

funnel

filter paper

dirty water

clean water

fingerprints

The pattern left by the ridges in the surface of the fingertips. The patterns are classified as arches, loops, whorls, or composite.

arch   loop   whorl   composite

fire

The product of something burning. Fire includes heat, light, flame, smoke, and fumes.

fire extinguisher

A device used to put out a fire. It usually works by cooling the fire or by excluding oxygen from the fire.

fish

A cold-blooded animal with a backbone that lives in water and breathes through gills. There are two main groups of fish. The bony fishes have a skeleton made of bone, for example, salmon and flounder. The cartilaginous fishes have a skeleton of cartilage, for example, sharks and rays.

See *bone, cartilage.*

flame

A "tongue" of fire; a flickering glow produced when something burns.

See *fire.*

flight

The process of moving through the air without touching the ground, as in bird or space flight.

float

To be supported by water or other liquid or gas, as in "the boat floats in the water" or "the balloon floats through the air."

flora

Referring to all the plant species in a particular area, as in "the flora of North America."

flower

The part of a flowering plant that contains the reproductive organs. Seeds develop in the ovary when the flower is fertilized.

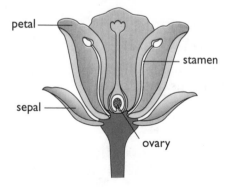

petal — stamen — sepal — ovary

See *blossom, fertilize.*

fluid

Any substance that can flow, for example, liquids and gases.

See *gas, liquid.*

fly

An animal with no backbone, of the insect order Diptera; an insect with only one pair of wings.

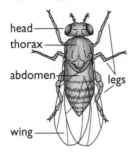

head
thorax
abdomen
legs
wing

See *insect*.

fog

Cloud or mist at ground level caused by moist air meeting cold air. Caused, for example, when air moves over the sea and meets cold land surface, or when warm air from the land rises during a clear night.

food chain

The feeding relationships between organisms in an area.

force

That which changes the shape or motion of objects, such as a push, pull, stretch, squash, or blow.

push

squash

pull

blow

stretch

forensic science

The science used to help solve crime. May include fingerprinting, blood testing, and voice identification. Computers are widely used to assist in forensic science.

forest

A large collection of growing trees; a woodland or jungle.

fossil

Preserved remains of plants or animals that lived long ago.

Dying fish falls to bottom of sea

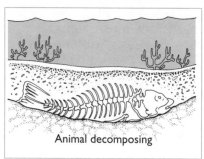
Animal decomposing

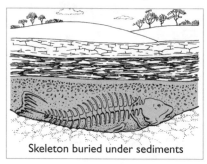
Skeleton buried under sediments

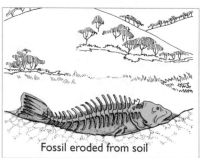
Fossil eroded from soil

How a fossil is formed

fossil fuel

Fuels such as coal, natural gas, and petroleum. Made from the remains of plants and animal bodies buried underground. Most fossil fuels are formed from life that existed about 300 million years ago (Carboniferous period).

See *coal, natural gas, Appendix III.*

fracture

A break or crack, such as of glass or a human bone.

freeze

To turn a liquid or gas to a solid by cooling it, for example, freezing water to make ice.

freezing point

The temperature at which a liquid turns to a solid. Water turns from a liquid to a solid (ice) at zero degrees Celsius (0°C) or 32 degrees Fahrenheit (32°F).

See *freeze.*

friction

A force that resists movement. Produced when two surfaces are rubbed against each other, for example, car tires and road surface.

See *force.*

frog

A cold-blooded animal with a backbone and smooth, moist skin. A frog spends part of its life on land and part in water.

See *amphibian, cold-blooded, tadpole.*

frond

The leafy part of ferns, palms, and algae.

See *algae, fern.*

frost

Ice deposited on the ground and other exposed surfaces when water in the atmosphere freezes. Frosts occur when the temperature drops below the freezing point.

See *freeze.*

fruit

Fleshy parts of plants containing seeds, some of which can be used as food.

fuel

Material that can be used to produce energy by burning. Food is the fuel of our bodies.

See *fossil fuel.*

fulcrum

The pivot point around which a lever works.

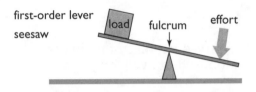

first-order lever
seesaw

load   fulcrum   effort

See *lever.*

fungus

A member of a group of living things that gain food by breaking down other living things. Fungi are placed in a kingdom separate from plants. They do not have leaves or roots. They reproduce by spores. Fungi include mushrooms, toadstools, yeasts, and molds.

See *kingdom.*

fur

Thick, fluffy hair on the outer layer of the skin of mammals. Fur keeps mammals warm. Fur has long been used by people as clothing. Human hair is a form of fur.

galaxy

Groups of billions of stars held together by gravity. The Earth's solar system is part of a galaxy known as the Milky Way.

See *Milky Way.*

gall bladder

A sac attached to the liver in humans. It receives and stores bile which helps to digest foods.

See *digestive system.*

gas

Airlike substance (not solid or liquid) in the form of fumes, air, or water vapor. Gas moves freely to fill any space available.

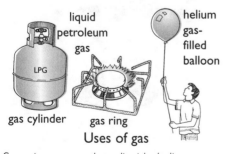

Uses of gas

See *air, argon, carbon dioxide, helium, hydrogen, natural gas, nitrogen, oxygen.*

gear

Wheels with "teeth" or cogs that turn other wheels with "teeth" to change their speed or direction.

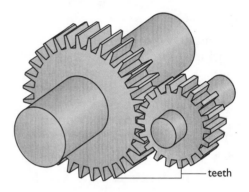

gemstone

A jewel; precious stone that is valued for hardness, rarity, and beauty. Examples include agate, amethyst, diamond, jade, lapis lazuli, sapphire, and tiger eye.

See *agate, amethyst, diamond, jade.*

gene

A unit of material inherited from our parents that determines a trait such as eye color, face shape, or hair color. We pass our genes on to our children.

See *chromosome, DNA, inherit.*

generator

A machine that converts mechanical energy into electrical energy.

See *motor.*

genetics

The study of genes and heredity.

See *gene, heredity*.

genus

The name for a group of species sharing common characteristics. For example, the genus "Panthera" is used for naming the lion species, *Panthera leo*; *Panthera tigris*, the tiger; *Panthera onca*, the jaguar; and *Panthera pardus*, the leopard.

See *scientific name, species, taxonomy*.

geology

The study of the formation, composition, and structure of the earth.

germ

(i) The part of a seed that will develop into a plant.

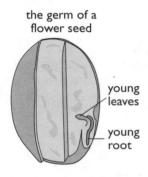

the germ of a
flower seed

young leaves

young root

(ii) A common term for disease agents such as viruses and bacteria.

See *seed*.

germinate

To sprout or start to grow roots, stems, and leaves from the germ in a seed or a spore.

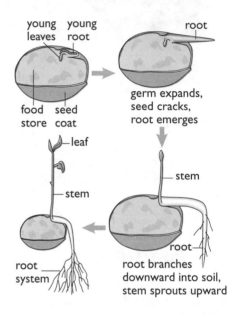

young leaves   young root

root

food store   seed coat

germ expands, seed cracks, root emerges

leaf

stem

stem

root

root system

root branches downward into soil, stem sprouts upward

See *germ, spore*.

gills

(i) Breathing organs in aquatic animals.
(ii) Frilled parts underneath the caps of some fungi.

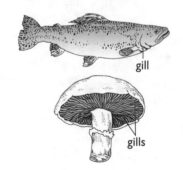

gill

gills

glacier

A mass of ice and snow that moves very slowly down a mountain or valley.

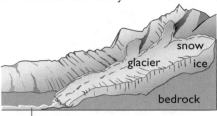

stream formed
by melting ice

globe

A round ball-shaped model of planet Earth.

globe of Earth

gold

A precious, malleable metal, yellow in color. Gold does not corrode easily. Gold has many uses, including coating surfaces with a thin layer of gold (gilding) and making jewelry.

See *metal*.

gradient

The steepness of a road or path.

See *incline, slope*.

granite

Coarse grained igneous rock mainly composed of quartz, mica, and felspar.

See *igneous rock, rock*.

grass

One of many green plants with blades, leaves, or stalks with grain-like fruits. Includes most cereal crop plants, such as wheat and rye.

gravity

The force of attraction between two objects. We experience it as a pull of things toward the center of the earth.

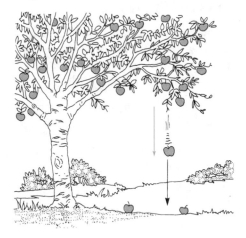

See *mass, weight*.

greenhouse effect

A term used to describe the increase in the temperature caused by the earth's atmosphere trapping heat from the sun. Similar effect to the way in which glass in a plant greenhouse traps the heat.

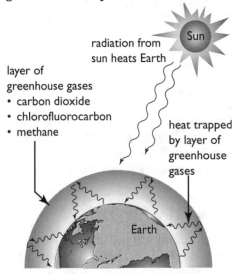

radiation from sun heats Earth

Sun

layer of greenhouse gases
• carbon dioxide
• chlorofluorocarbon
• methane

heat trapped by layer of greenhouse gases

Earth

gyroscope

A rotating wheel inside a frame. Once the wheel is set in motion, it resists any change of direction even when the base of the gyroscope is moved. Used in a ship's instrumentation to help keep the ship on course.

growth

Development; general increase in size. For example, a human being develops from an infant, to a child, to an adolescent, to an adult.

grub

The larva of an insect such as a moth and a beetle.

See *caterpillar, larva.*

habitat

A place where plants or animals live and which provides for all their needs. Most habitats are home to many different plants and animals.

hail

Rain in the form of ice. Hail is formed when raindrops are driven upward by air currents and freeze.

See *freeze, snow.*

hair

Fine threads growing from the skin of animals in the group called mammals, which includes humans. A type of fur.

See *fur, mammal.*

Halley's comet

The brightest comet seen from Earth. It is named after Edmund Halley who worked out its orbit. The comet orbits the sun every 76 years. It will next be seen from Earth in 2061.

See *comet.*

hardware

(i) A tool, a part of a machine, or a fastener made of metal.

(ii) A physical component of a computer (for example, a hard drive, monitor, or keyboard) or an accessory to a computer (for example, a modem, printer, or scanner).

hatch

To be born from an egg. For example, birds and lizards hatch from eggs.

hazard label

A standard symbol that indicates or warns of possible dangers.

corrosive explosive

flammable harmful/irritant toxic

head

(i) In animals, the front or top body part above the neck that contains the brain, eyes, nose, and mouth.

(ii) Top part of any object such as the head of a hammer, the head of a bolt.

(iii) The part in tape players that reads the coded message.

hearing

The sensing of sound.

See *ear*.

heart

The muscular organ that pumps blood around the body of animals.

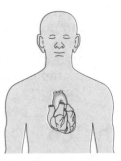

In humans, the heart is located in the chest cavity.

heartbeat

The regular pumping action of the heart.

See *heart, pulse*.

heat

A form of energy. Heat flows from objects that are hotter to those that are colder. It is sensed by the skin as warmth. Heat is measured in calories or joules.

height

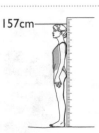

157cm

The distance that can be measured from the top to the bottom.

helium

The lightest inert gas. It is the second most common element in the universe. Most stars contain helium.

See *gas, inert*.

hematology

The study of blood, especially through the use of chemical tests and microscopes.

See *blood*.

hemisphere

Half a sphere. The earth is a sphere that is divided by the equator into Northern and Southern Hemispheres.

See *equator*.

hemophilia

Inherited diseases of the blood in which the blood does not clot.

See *blood*.

herb

(i) Any plant used as flavoring in cooking or as a medicine. Examples are parsley, mint, rosemary, and sage.

(ii) Any plant with a nonwoody stem that dies down after flowering.

herbicide

A chemical poison that kills plants. Weeds and other unwanted or invasive plants can be sprayed with herbicides to control their spread.

herbivore

An animal that feeds on plants; examples include deer, rabbits, horses, elephants, and pigeons.

heredity

The passing on of characteristics from parents to their offspring.
See *inherit.*

hibernate

To slow down body processes during winter, as seen in many animals such as bears and toads living in cold zones.

hinge

A moveable joint connecting two things, such as a door to a door frame. The elbow is an example of a hinge joint in the body.

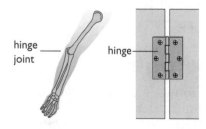

See *joint, skeleton.*

hip

The area of the body where the leg bones meet the pelvis.
See *joint, skeleton.*

histology

The study of cells and tissues of living things.
See *cell.*

hologram

A three-dimensional picture produced with laser lights.
See *laser.*

horizon

The line at which the sky and ground or sea seem to meet. To a person standing at sea level, the horizon is about 5 kilometers away.

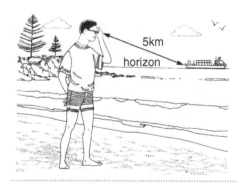

hormone

A substance produced by a gland that is carried by the bloodstream to specific organs and/or tissues in the body. Hormones influence the activities of their target organs. Human growth hormone is produced by the pituitary gland. Growth hormone stimulates the growth of muscle and bone.

Hubble space telescope

An optical telescope, 2.5 meters in diameter, placed in orbit above Earth in April 1990. It can observe distant galaxies much better than any telescope on Earth because it does not observe through Earth's atmosphere. It can send the information it collects back to Earth. It is named after American astronomer Edwin Hubble.

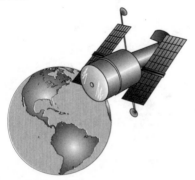

humidity

The measure of moisture in the air.
See *weather*.

humus

Black or dark-brown material that comes from the breaking down of organic matter in the upper layer of soil. Humus provides nutrients for plant growth.
See *compost, soil*.

hurricane

A wind of force 12 on the Beaufort wind scale. A severe storm wind.
See *Beaufort wind scale*.

hybrid

Offspring from the sexual union of different varieties or breeds of the same species or from two different species. When hybrids from the same species reproduce, they do not breed "true," and their offspring may not look like them. Hybrids from different species are sterile and unable to reproduce.
See *species*.

hydroelectric energy

Electrical energy generated by the movement of water.
See *water energy, renewable energy*.

hydrogen

The lightest element, given the symbol H. It is a colorless, odorless gas that is very reactive. Water is formed when hydrogen is combined with oxygen.
See *gas*.

hydroponics

A technique for growing plants
without soil. All the necessary
plant nutrients usually provided by
soil are delivered to the plants in
water. The roots of the plants can
be in water or held by gravel,
sand, or another substance.

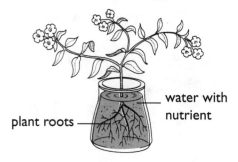

plant roots ⎯⎯⎯   water with
                 nutrient

hypothesis

An idea about an event that can
be explained by means of a test. A
scientific guess based on evidence.

ice

Frozen water, made solid, as in ice cubes. Pure water freezes at 0 degrees Celsius or 32 degrees Fahrenheit. Ice is crystal-like, brittle, and transparent. Water expands when it freezes.

ice age

A period when sheets of ice covered large parts of continents on earth. There have been many ice ages in the earth's past.

Ice Ages of the Earth

Ice Age	Time	Continent
Pleistocene epoch	600,000 to 10,000 years ago	Northern Hemisphere
Permo carboniferous period	300 million years ago	Southern Hemisphere

iceberg

A mass of ice that has broken off from a glacier and is floating in the sea.

How icebergs form

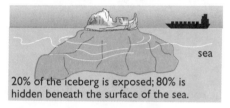

20% of the iceberg is exposed; 80% is hidden beneath the surface of the sea.

See *glacier*.

identify

To recognize or state the name of something, as in "I can identify living things."

igneous rock

Rock formed from molten (volcanic) rock. Rock cooled and hardened at the earth's surface or deep inside the crust of the earth.

See *rock, volcanic rock*.

image

The exact likeness of something, for example, a mirror image.

See *reflection*.

immature

Not mature, not developed.

See *life cycle*.

immunize

To protect against foreign micro-organisms. Medical scientists have developed substances that increase our ability to resist infection from particular diseases.

See *disease*.

implement

Any instrument or tool used for a particular purpose.

See *tool*.

incline

A slope, ramp.

inert

Not reacting chemically with other substances. Helium is an inert gas.

See *gas*.

infection

A disease caused by invasion of microorganisms, such as bacteria. Infection in a tooth is experienced as a toothache.

See *disease*.

infinity

A quantity that is larger than any that can be measured or counted. Increasing with no end. May be continued without ever coming to an end.

The symbol for infinity is .

infrared radiation

Electromagnetic radiation with wavelengths longer than the red part of the spectrum. These rays are not visible.

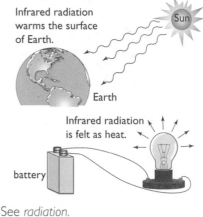

Infrared radiation warms the surface of Earth.

Sun

Earth

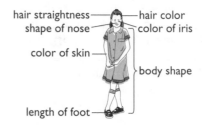

Infrared radiation is felt as heat.

battery

See *radiation*.

inhabit

To live in a particular area. Humans inhabit the earth; frogs inhabit freshwater habitats.

inherit

To receive traits and physical characteristics passed on by parents.

hair straightness — hair color
shape of nose — color of iris
color of skin —
body shape
length of foot —

insect

A small animal with no backbone. Its body is divided into three parts (head, thorax, abdomen), with three pairs of jointed legs. Many insects have one or two pairs of wings. Their bodies are covered by an exoskeleton. The young hatch from eggs. The fly, beetle, butterfly, and ant are examples of insects.

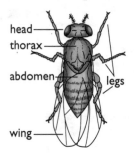

head
thorax
abdomen
legs
wing

See *arthropod, exoskeleton, invertebrate.*

instinct

Something an animal or a person is able to do without having to learn it. A worker bee flies to and from the hive by instinct. Some bird species fly to other areas at given times of the year by instinct.

instrument

A device or tool used for a particular purpose. There are instruments for medical purposes, for measuring, making sounds, and viewing things. A harp is a musical instrument. An air traffic controller uses radar and radio instruments.

See *tool.*

insulator

A poor conductor of heat, sound, or electricity.

battery

The plastic mug is an insulator; it does not conduct electricity.

The brick room keeps sound from escaping; brick is a good insulator.

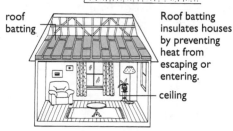

roof batting

Roof batting insulates houses by preventing heat from escaping or entering.

ceiling

See *conduction.*

Internet

A worldwide network of computers able to exchange data.

See *e-mail.*

intestine

A long tube in animals in which food is digested by separating nutrients and leaving the waste in the form of feces.

See *digestive system, large intestine, small intestine.*

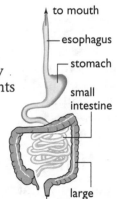

to mouth
esophagus
stomach
small intestine
large intestine
rectum

invention

(i) Something new devised by a person. Alexander Graham Bell invented the telephone in 1876.
(ii) The process of devising something new.

invertebrate

An animal without a backbone or spine, for example, a snail, spider, or worm.

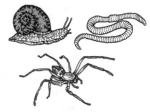

See *animal, vertebrate.*

investigate

To explore, research, and examine closely, as in "I will investigate the most suitable glues for joining two pieces of wood."

iodine

A widely occurring chemical. It is extracted from ashes of seaweed and made into a liquid. Used in medicine as an antiseptic.

ionosphere

A layer of the earth's atmosphere, stretching from 80 km (50 miles) above the earth's surface for many hundreds of kilometers (miles).

See *atmosphere.*

iris

The part of the eye that controls the amount of light entering the eye. In humans, the iris is the colored part of the eye.

See *eye.*

iron

(i) The most widely used of all metals. Iron is used in the making of many tools, structures, and machines. A cast-iron frying pan is one example.
(ii) A naturally occurring substance used by our bodies to make blood. Some foods are rich in iron.

See *metal.*

jack

A device used to raise heavy objects a short distance, for example, a car jack.

jade

Hard, semiprecious stone. Jade ranges in color from almost transparent to black. Pale green jade is usually the color used in making ornaments. Jade is rated around 5.5–5.6 on the Mohs scale of hardness.

See *gemstone, Mohs scale.*

jellyfish

An animal without a backbone that lives in the sea. Jellyfish have a bell-shaped, jellylike body with a fringe of tentacles. Jellyfish belong to the group called Coelenterates, which also includes corals and sea anemones.

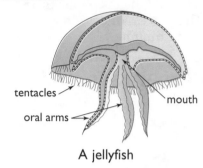

tentacles

oral arms

mouth

A jellyfish

joint

A structure connecting two bones together in the body, such as the hip joint or knee joint.

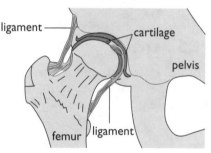

ligament

cartilage

pelvis

femur

ligament

See *bone.*

Jupiter

The fifth planet from the sun; the largest planet in our solar system.

See *solar system.*

juvenile

A young animal or plant.

See *life cycle.*

kidney

One of a pair of bean-shaped organs found in vertebrates; filters wastes from the blood and turns them into liquid waste.

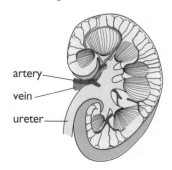

artery
vein
ureter

Cross section of a kidney

See *excretory system*.

kaleidoscope

An instrument with mirrors that are placed in a specific way to create symmetrical images. Colored objects at one end of the tube are reflected in the mirrors to make patterns.

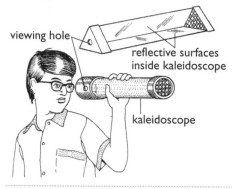

viewing hole
reflective surfaces inside kaleidoscope
kaleidoscope

kinetic energy

Energy possessed by moving objects.

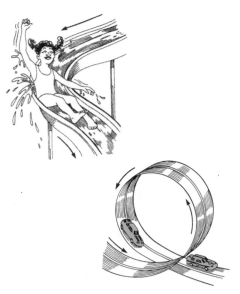

Examples of objects in motion

See *energy*.

keystone

A wedge-shaped block or stone at the top center point of an arch that holds the other blocks in place.

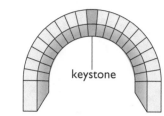

keystone

See *arch*.

kingdom

One of the five main groupings of living things on earth. All living things on earth are placed into one of these groups.

Kingdoms of Living Things

Animal kingdom	example: mouse
Plant kingdom	example: tree
Fungi kingdom	example: mushroom
Protists kingdom	example: algae
Monerans kingdom	example: bacteria

See *animal, bacteria, fungus, taxonomy, Appendix 1.*

knee

The joint between the lower leg and the upper leg in humans and other animals.

See *joint, skeleton.*

krill

Shrimplike crustaceans that live in cold oceans. Krill are an important food source for baleen whales.

See *crustacean.*

latitude

Lines drawn on the globe parallel to the equator. These imaginary lines are used with longitude to locate positions on the globe.

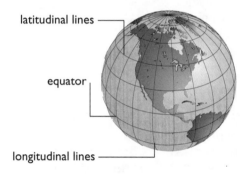

latitudinal lines

equator

longitudinal lines

See *equator, longitude.*

large intestine

The end part of the digestive system where water is absorbed from waste to form feces.

See *digestive system.*

larva

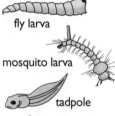

fly larva

mosquito larva

tadpole

The stage of the life cycle in some animals between hatching and adult. Examples include the tadpole stage of frogs, the maggot stage of flies, and the caterpillar stage of insects. The process by which larvae change to adults is called metamorphosis.

lava

Hot molten rock that erupts from a volcano.

See *volcano.*

leaf

The outgrowth from the stems of plants. A leaf has a stalk and a blade. The leaf is the main organ for producing food in plants. Leaves take many shapes and patterns.

laser

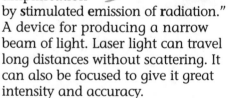

Short for "light amplification by stimulated emission of radiation." A device for producing a narrow beam of light. Laser light can travel long distances without scattering. It can also be focused to give it great intensity and accuracy.

See *light.*

leap year

A year that has an extra day added to the calendar. A leap year has 366 days. Leap years occur every four years. In a leap year the extra day is added to February. February normally has 28 days; in a leap year it has 29 days.

lens

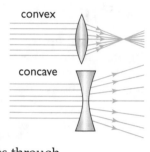
convex

concave

A piece of transparent material, such as glass or plastic, that causes light to bend when it passes through.

lever

A simple machine consisting of a beam pivoted at a point called the fulcrum. Levers are described as first-, second-, or third-order levers, according to the position of the fulcrum and the load. Many tools use levers to make work easier.

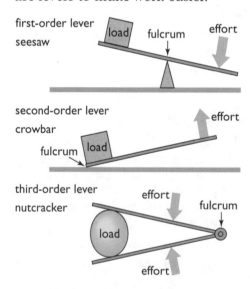

first-order lever
seesaw
load   fulcrum   effort

second-order lever
crowbar
fulcrum   load   effort

third-order lever
nutcracker
effort   fulcrum
load
effort

lichen

Living things that grow on the surface of rocks, logs, and soil, creating a flat, crusty, green-grey patch. Lichen are formed when a fungus and an alga live together.

life

The ability to grow and reproduce. See *living thing*.

life cycle

Stages through which living things pass, usually shown as a circle.

Human life cycle

Butterfly life cycle

Plant life cycle

lift

(i) To raise.
(ii) The force that supports aircraft in flight.
(iii) A device with a platform for moving things up and down, for example, an elevator in a multistory building.

See *aerodynamics, thrust.*

light

A form of energy sensed by the eyes; the visible part of electromagnetic radiation. Sunlight is made up of light beams of different colors. Light travels at a speed of about 186,000 miles per second.

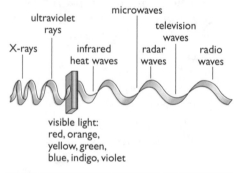

ultraviolet rays
microwaves
television waves
X-rays
infrared heat waves
radar waves
radio waves

visible light: red, orange, yellow, green, blue, indigo, violet

light bulb

A device that emits light when electricity is passed through it.

See *globe.*

lightning

Sudden brilliant flash of light in the sky caused by the discharge of built-up electrical charge in the atmosphere.

light-year

The distance light travels in space in one year (about 9.4 trillion kilometers). Used in astronomy to measure large distances.

Brightest Star Distances in Light-Years

Sun	0.000015 (140,000,000 kilometers)
Sirius	8.6
Canopus	1200
Alpha Centuari A	4.5
Achenar	85

limestone

Sedimentary rock composed mainly of the shells of marine organisms.

See *rock.*

liquid

Material that takes the shape of the container it is in and forms a level surface; the state of matter between a gas and a solid.

liver

A large organ found in animals. In vertebrates it is located in the abdomen. It aids in digestion of foods.

See *digestive system.*

living thing

Any of the wide range of things having the attributes of life—being able to grow, reproduce, and respond to stimuli. Living things are classified by scientists into kingdoms.

See *kingdom*.

lizard

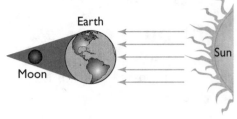

An animal with a backbone, a scaly body, and four legs, which is from the group called reptiles.

See *reptile*.

load

A weight to be supported or moved.

See *lever*.

loam

Soil that is a mixture of sand, silt, and clay.

See *soil*.

locomotion

The ability to move from one place to another, as when walking, flying, or swimming.

lodestone

A form of rock called magnetite that acts as a magnet.

See *magnetite*.

longitude

Lines drawn on the globe at right angles to latitude lines. These imaginary lines are used with latitude to locate positions on the globe.

See *latitude*.

lubricate

To add a substance to reduce friction between moving surfaces. Grease and oil are commonly used to lubricate moving parts.

See *friction*.

lunar eclipse

When the moon passes into the shadow of the earth.

Lunar eclipse

See *eclipse*, *solar eclipse*.

lung

One of a pair of organs in the chest used for breathing.

See *respiratory system*.

machine

A device used to do work; usually referring to things made up of a number of parts.

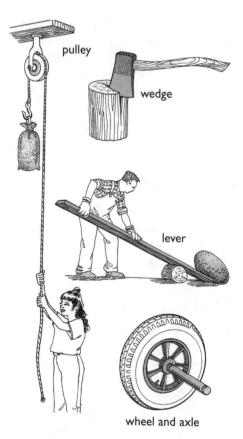

pulley

wedge

lever

wheel and axle

Examples of simple machines

maggot

A small, white, wormlike grub that hatches from the egg of an insect, such as the fly.

See *fly, larva.*

magma

Hot molten rock under the crust of the earth's surface.

See *lava, volcano.*

magnet

A piece of metal that attracts objects made from iron.

magnetite

Magnetic, raw iron ore. Used to make magnets.

See *magnet.*

magnifier

A lens used to make things look larger.

mammal

A member of the class of warm-blooded vertebrate animals. Mammals have body hair, and their young feed on the milk of their mother. Monkeys, whales, horses, dogs, goats, and humans are all mammals.

mammoth

One of many species of large extinct elephants. The woolly mammoth had a hairy covering and long curved tusks. Evidence of mammoths is found worldwide. Early people hunted mammoths for food.

mantle

A layer of rocks between the crust and the core of the earth. It is partly solid and partly liquid, like a thick paste. It is very hot and always moving. This layer ranges in depth from 40 to 3,480 km.

See *earthquake.*

manufacture

To make objects by hand or machine, sometimes on a large scale.

Manufacturing process

marble

A metamorphic rock formed when limestone is changed under heat and pressure. Marble has attractive textures and colors. It can be cut and polished and is often used for making statues and as a building material.

See *metamorphic rock, rock.*

Mars

The fourth planet from the sun.

See *solar system.*

marsupial

The order of mammals in which the young are born and move to a pouch where they drink their mother's milk. Most marsupials are native to Australia. The kangaroo, koala, possum, and wombat are all marsupials.

mass

The quantity of matter that a body contains. Mass is pulled upon by gravity in such a way that the more mass a body has the more it weighs. Although weight does not exist without gravity, mass stays the same with or without it.

See *gravity, weight.*

material

Anything of which something is made, for example, bricks, glass, wood, leather, tin. Refers especially to cloth.

matter

Anything that takes up space and can be weighed. Three states of matter are solid, liquid, and gas.

gas

solid   liquid

States of matter

See *gas, liquid, solid.*

measure

To find out the size or amount of something, such as its weight or height.

Measuring devices

medicine

(i) The study, treatment, and prevention of disease.
(ii) Any substance used to treat disease.

See *disease.*

megaphone

A large funnel-shaped instrument used to make sound louder.

melt

To change from a solid to a liquid, usually through heating, for example, ice at room temperature melts to water.

mercury

White, silvery metal. Liquid at room temperature. Used in some thermometers and barometers.

See *metal.*

Mercury

The closest planet to the sun.

See *solar system.*

metabolism

The total of all processes by which a living organism stays alive. In human beings, metabolism includes respiration, digestion, growth, and repair.

See *growth.*

metal

Any one of a group of chemical substances that includes aluminum, gold, iron, mercury, silver, steel, and zinc. Most are grey or silver. Most metals are good conductors of heat and electricity. Metals expand when heated and contract when cooled.

Metal	Properties	Used in the manufacture of
aluminum	Good conductor of electricity Light in weight	Kitchen foil Saucepans Building and construction
copper	Good conductor of electricity Malleable	Electrical wire Water pipes
iron	Tough and hard Can be cast, forged, machined, rolled	Building and construction Tools Machinery Steel
mercury	Liquid at room temperature Poisonous	Thermometers Electric switches
silver	Good conductor of electricity Malleable	Coins Jewelry Photography Medicine Batteries
zinc	Prevents rusting Combines with other metals	Coats iron and steel Bronze=zinc+copper +tin Brass=zinc+copper Batteries

See *aluminum, bronze, copper, gold, iron, mercury, steel, zinc.*

metamorphic rock

Changed rock; volcanic or sedimentary rock changed from its original form by heat or pressure.

Changes in Rock

Rock		Changes to
limestone	heated →	marble
limestone	pressurized →	quartzite
shale	heated →	slate
shale	pressurized →	schist

See *rock, sedimentary rock, volcanic rock.*

metamorphosis

The change from one form or shape of an animal to another, especially of an immature form to an adult form, for example, a frog changing from tadpole to adult frog.

See *life cycle.*

meteor

A small mass of rock and metal moving around the sun. Also known as dwarf planets. Meteors light up when passing through Earth's atmosphere, resembling falling stars. Commonly called "shooting stars."

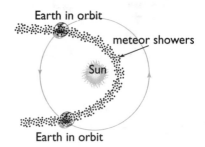

Meteor showers

meteorology

The study of weather and climate.

See *climate, weather.*

microorganism

Living things that can only be seen with a microscope, such as bacteria and viruses. Also referred to as microbes. Includes most single-celled organisms.

microphone

A device that changes sound waves into electrical waves. Sound waves are sent along wires to loudspeakers. Used when recording sounds or making sounds louder.

microphone

microscope

A device with lenses that are used to make small objects appear larger. Used to identify and study microorganisms.

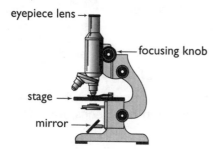

eyepiece lens →
← focusing knob
stage →
mirror →

See *microorganism*.

migrate

To move from one area to another. Many animals move location according to seasons. For example, some birds migrate between the Northern and Southern Hemispheres in search of warmer weather.

Milky Way

The galaxy in which Earth is located. Resembles a spiral.

See *galaxy*.

millipede

An arthropod with many legs. It has two pairs of legs per segment.

See *arthropod*.

mineral

A natural substance found in the earth's crust. Minerals are made up of substances that were never alive. Atoms of a mineral are crystalline.

Mineral	Mineral hardness	Used to make
talc	1	talcum powder, chalk
graphite	1–2	pencil lead
gypsum	2	plaster of Paris
diamond	10	jewelery

Some minerals, their hardness, and their uses

See *metal, Mohs scale*.

mirage

An optical illusion caused by atmospheric conditions. A person may see an object that appears to be in the distance, such as a sheet of water on a hot road or in a desert.

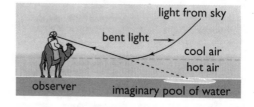

light from sky
bent light →
cool air
hot air
observer
imaginary pool of water

mirror

Any shiny surface that reflects light. Usually refers to a sheet of glass that is coated with silvery paint on its back surface and that reflects an image; examples include a bathroom mirror and a car's rearview mirror.

mixture

The product of two or more substances mixed together but not chemically joined. Mixtures can be separated through physical means such as filtering, freezing, melting, or distilling.

See *compound*.

modem

A device that allows computers to connect to other computers using telephone lines.

See *hardware*.

Mohs scale

A scale for classifying the relative hardness of minerals.

Mineral hardness	Common examples of hardness
10 diamond	scratches all natural materials
9 corundum 8 topaz 7 quartz 6 orthoclase	scratches a penknife blade or window glass
5 apatite 4 fluorite	scratched by a penknife blade or window glass
3 calcite	scratched by a copper coin
2 gypsum 1 talc	scratched by a fingernail

See *mineral*.

mold

Fungus. Furry growth that develops and grows in damp conditions. Molds can ruin foods such as cheese, bread, and fruit.

molecule

The smallest particle into which a substance can be divided, consisting of one or more atoms.

See *atom*.

mollusk

An animal with no backbone. It has a soft body and no segments.

See *slug, snail*.

monotreme

A type of mammal in which the young hatch from eggs, for example, the platypus.

moon

A satellite of a planet that shines by reflected light of the sun. Earth's moon moves around Earth once every 29.5 days.

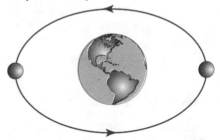

The moon orbits Earth in an oval-shaped path (ellipse).

See *satellite*.

moss

A small, soft, green, nonflowering plant that reproduces from spores. Clumps of moss grow in damp places as soft dense mats on rocks, wood, or soil and at the base of trees.

See *spore*.

motion

Change of position. Movement.

motor

A machine that uses fuel or electricity to make other things work.

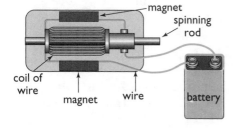

Electrical energy is changed to mechanical energy in a motor.

mouth

The cavelike opening to the digestive system through which food is received. In humans the mouth contains the tongue and teeth. Saliva is produced by glands located near the mouth.

See *digestive system, saliva*.

muscle

Body tissue or organ that can contract and relax. Muscles cause parts of the body to move.

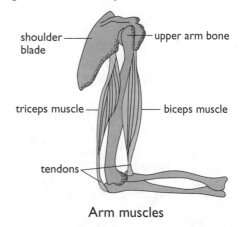

Arm muscles

mushroom

The common name for the edible gill fungus.

See *fungus*.

nerve, nerve fiber

A strand of tissue that carries signals between the brain and other parts of the body; extension of a nerve cell body that occurs in the brain and spinal cord.

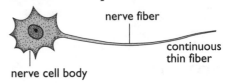

nerve fiber

continuous thin fiber

nerve cell body

See *nervous system.*

natural gas

Any gas found in the earth's crust. Natural gas is a fossil fuel. It is often found with petroleum.

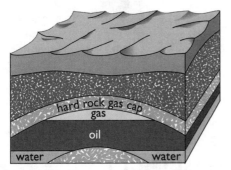

hard rock gas cap
gas
oil
water   water

See *fossil fuel, gas.*

nervous system

Parts of an animal's body that control all the body's activity. In higher animals the nervous system is made up of the brain, spinal cord, and nerve fibers extending to all parts of the body.

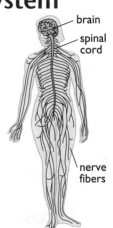

brain

spinal cord

nerve fibers

natural selection

The process by which those organisms that are best adapted to their environment have a better chance of surviving and passing their genetic characteristics on to their offspring.

Neptune

The eighth planet in the solar system. Discovered in 1846. Neptune can only be seen with a telescope.

See *solar system.*

night

The part of the 24-hour daily cycle when an area of the earth is in darkness. The area facing away from the sun is in night.

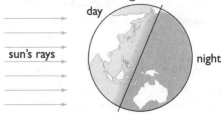

day

sun's rays

night

See *day.*

nitrogen

A colorless and odorless gas that makes up about 80 percent of the earth's atmosphere.

See *atmosphere, gas.*

nocturnal

Referring to being active at night. Many hunting animals are nocturnal, for example, the owl, the fox, and the cat.

nose

The upper part of the respiratory system and the sense organ of smell.

See *respiratory system.*

nostril

One of the two openings of the nose in which the sense receptors for smell are located. Air enters the body through the nostrils when an animal is breathing.

See *nose.*

nuclear energy

Energy generated from changes in the nucleus of atoms.

See *energy.*

nucleus

(i) The central core of atoms containing most of their mass. A nucleus consists of protons and neutrons.

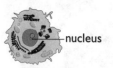
nucleus

See *atom.*

(ii) The control center of cells.

nucleus

See *cell.*

nutrition

Referring to the way living things obtain the fuel or food they need to live and grow, for example, plants use the sun's energy to make their food. Animals eat other living things to obtain food.

nylon

A synthetic fiber; the first such fiber to be made, in 1938. It is made using petroleum, natural gas, air, and water.

See *synthetic.*

nymph

A stage in the life cycle of insects such as grasshoppers and dragonflies. These insects do not have a pupa phase. Nymphs look similar to the adult but have no wings or reproductive organs.

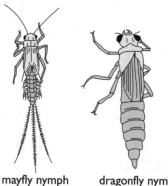

mayfly nymph   dragonfly nymph

See *life cycle, pupa.*

observatory

A building that houses telescopes for observing planets, stars, and weather patterns.

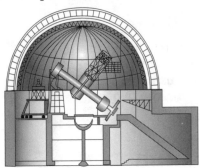

observe

To see, hear, touch, taste, or smell something, as in "I can observe life around me by looking, listening, smelling, tasting, and touching."

ocean

A large area of salt water, for example, Atlantic Ocean, Pacific Ocean. Oceans cover approximately three-quarters of the earth's surface.

octopus

A sea creature with a soft oval body and eight tentacles with suckers. They belong to the invertebrate animal group of mollusk.

See *mollusk.*

offspring

Referring to the young of a particular animal. A calf is the offspring of a cow; a kitten is the offspring of a cat.

oil

(i) Fatty liquid made from vegetable or animal fats. Often used in cooking.
(ii) Thick, black liquid made from petroleum and used to lubricate machinery.

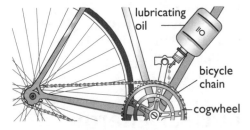

Oiling a chain

See *lubricate.*

omnivore

A term used to describe animals that eat many kinds of food, including plants and animals. People and many small mammals are described as omnivores.

See *carnivore, herbivore.*

opaque

Not transmitting light. Unable to be seen through. A block of wood, muddy water, and a metal can are examples of opaque objects.

optical fiber

A thin glass rod. The inside walls of the rod act like mirrors. Light passes through the rod and travels out the other end. Optical fibers are much lighter than copper wire. Used to transmit information.

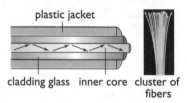

plastic jacket

cladding glass   inner core   cluster of fibers

Inside walls act like mirrors.

optical illusion

Something that deceives or tricks the eye by giving a false impression.

A   B

Horizontal lines are of equal length, but line A appears longer than line B.

orbit

The curved path of a body in space around another, for example, the path of a planet around the sun or a satellite around a planet.

See *asteroid, moon, solar system.*

organ

(i)   A musical instrument with a keyboard. Pipe organs produce sound using pipes, such as those seen in large cathedrals. Electronic organs produce sound using electricity.

(ii)   Part of the body of an animal or plant; has a particular function. In animals, organs include the brain, heart, liver, and lungs. A leaf is a plant organ.

See *brain, heart, kidney, liver, lung, stomach.*

organism

A complete living thing made up of parts that work together to carry out the processes of life. Some organisms are small and consist of only one cell. Others consist of many cells, tissues, organs, and systems.

ovum

The correct term for "egg."

See *egg.*

oxygen

A gas that is tasteless, odorless, and colorless. It makes up 21 percent of the earth's atmosphere. Animals breathe in oxygen. Plants make oxygen when they produce food.

ozone

A gas; a form of oxygen. Ozone is produced by lightning flashes in the upper atmosphere. Ozone filters some of the sun's rays.

Lightning changes some oxygen in the earth's upper atmosphere to ozone.

See *atmosphere, lightning, oxygen.*

paleontology

The study of fossil animals and plants. The study includes their structure, how they changed with time, and how they lived.

See *fossil*.

pancreas

An organ of the digestive system, connected to the small intestine. The pancreas produces chemicals for digestion of food and control of sugar levels in the blood.

See *digestive system*.

paper

Sheets of flexible material made from webs of vegetable fibers such as wood pulp and rags. Paper is made by mixing fibers with water to create thin sheets. These sheets are then dried and hardened. Used for writing, printing, and wrapping, and for general household use, for example, tissue paper, paper towels.

parachute

An umbrella of fabric designed to slow the drop of a falling object. It is made of silk or nylon and has a system of ropes.

parasite

A living thing that lives on or in another, feeding from it. It gives nothing in return to the host. A flea is a parasite that lives on dogs, cats, and humans and sucks their blood for food.

pasteurize

A process used to kill micro-organisms in milk (or other substances) by heating. Milk is pasteurized by heating it to about 65 degrees Celsius for 30 minutes and then sealing the container airtight. The process is named after Louis Pasteur. He showed that souring of milk was caused by microscopic organisms in the air.

pendulum

A weight, called a bob, fixed to the end of a string that is held in a fixed position. The pendulum swings freely to and fro.

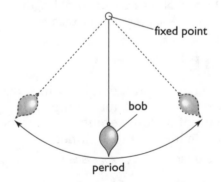

A swinging pendulum

percussion

A group of musical instruments that make sound by striking or by clashing together. A drum and cymbals are percussion instruments.

perennial

Plants that live for more than two years. Most flower each year. Annuals, in contrast, develop from seed and die each year.

pesticide

Chemicals applied to crops to kill pests.

pH

The measure of acid in a liquid. On the pH scale, water is neutral at pH 7. A pH below 7 is acidic. A pH above 7 is alkaline.

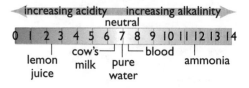

See *acid, alkaline.*

photosynthesis

A chemical process in green plants in which light energy is used to make food for the plant. This food is in the form of a carbohydrate such as starch.

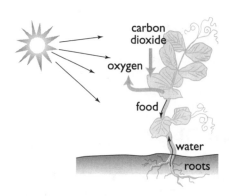

physics

The study of physical changes in matter caused by the effects of energy. Physics includes the study of movement, heat, light, magnetism, electricity, and sound.
See *energy.*

pitch

The frequency of sound waves. Low-pitch sounds have low freqency; high-pitch sounds have high frequency.
See *sound.*

planet

An object in space that orbits around a star. Earth and the other planets in the solar system are visible because they reflect the sun's light. They do not generate light and heat.
See *solar system.*

planetarium

A building or device in which the pattern of the stars can be observed.

plankton

Animals and plants that float in watery environments; usually microscopic in size.

plant

A living thing that produces its own food through photosynthesis. Includes seed plants, ferns, mosses, and algae.

See *anatomy, photosynthesis.*

plasma

The watery fluid of the blood in which the blood cells are suspended.
See *blood.*

plastics

A range of synthetic materials that are light, strong, and flexible. Examples of plastic items are household buckets, jugs, garden furniture, brushes, combs, and soft drink bottles.

Pluto

The ninth planet from the sun.
See *solar system.*

pole

One end of a magnet.
See *magnet.*

pollen

Fine powder produced by the male parts of flowering plants.
See *flower.*

population

The number of organisms of the same species living together in a specified area.

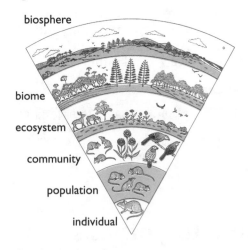

biosphere

biome

ecosystem

community

population

individual

See *biome, biosphere, community, ecosystem.*

predator

An animal that hunts and eats other animals (called its prey).

Prey   Predator

snail   seagull

lizard   eagle

gazelle   leopard

small dinosaur   large dinosaur

prey

Animals hunted and eaten by predators.

See *predator.*

primate

A group of mammals that includes lemurs, apes, monkeys, and humans. Primates have long, grasping hands and feet with long fingers and toes.

prism

A transparent solid that bends rays of light. A prism breaks up white light into the colors of the spectrum.

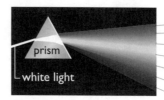

red (shortest in prism)
orange
yellow
prism
green
white light
blue
indigo
violet

See *spectrum.*

producer

An organism that produces food for itself. Plants are producers. They use sunlight and carbon dioxide to create their food supplies.

projectile

An object thrown or fired using force.

propeller

A device of spinning blades that drives an aircraft or ship.

protein

Large molecules made of smaller units called amino acids. Amino acids are made of carbon, nitrogen, hydrogen, and oxygen. Different parts of the human body are made of protein molecules assembled from the amino acids in the foods we eat. Skin, nails, hair, and connective tissues are made of protein.

proton

One of the three basic building blocks of matter. It is a positively charged particle in the nucleus of atoms.

See *atom*.

protozoa

Single-celled animals.

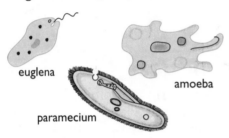

Examples of protozoa

pulley

A system for raising heavy loads, consisting of a wheel with grooves in which to slide a rope or chain.

pulse

The regular beating in the arteries as blood is pumped into them by the heart.

See *circulatory system, heartbeat*.

pupa

A stage in the life cycle of insects that undergo metamorphosis.

See *metamorphosis*.

pupil

The opening in the center of the eye through which light can enter the eye. In humans the pupil appears as a black circle.

See *eye*.

quartz

A common mineral that occurs in many types of rock. Pure quartz is colorless and transparent.

See *crystal, mineral, Mohs scale, rock.*

radar

Stands for **ra**dio **d**etection **a**nd **r**anging: a system to detect objects such as cars, ships, and planes at a distance by bouncing radio waves off them.

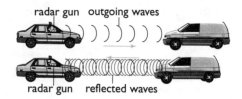

radar gun   outgoing waves

radar gun   reflected waves

radiation

The sending out of energy in all directions. Most often used to describe electromagnetic radiation, for example, light in rays traveling in all directions from its source. A candle radiates light from its flame.

See *electromagnetic spectrum.*

radioactive

The property of a substance with an unstable nucleus that results in the release of energy. Uranium is an example of a radioactive substance.

radius

(i) One of the bones in the arm of an animal.

See *skeleton*.

(ii) A line segment from the center of a circle or sphere to a point on the circle or sphere.

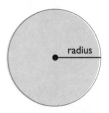

rain

Water formed when vapor in clouds condenses into droplets and falls from the sky.

Droplets inside the cloud join together to form bigger drops. When they are large and heavy enough they fall as rain.

Millions of droplets form a cloud.

Water vapor rises into cold air, condenses into small drops of water.

See *vapor*.

rainbow

An arc of the colors of the spectrum, seen in the sky when sun shines through rain.

raindrops

light rays

sun

rainforest

Dense forest found in hot areas with high rainfall, such as those near the equator.

rare (species)

Describing species that are under threat because they are low in numbers or occur in only a few places.

See *endangered, species*.

ray

(i) A narrow beam, for example, of visible light.

(ii) A kind of fish related to sharks, with a broad flattened body. It has a skeleton of cartilage.

See *cartilage*.

rayon

A synthetic fabric with silky texture made from plant fibers.

See *synthetic*.

reaction

An action in response to another action.

(i) A movement in response to a force, for example, how a cart reacts when pushed.

(ii) In chemistry, a chemical change, for example, how water reacts when heated.

See *chemical reaction*.

(iii) An animal response to a stimulus, for example, pulling one's hand away when it is burned.

recycle

To change used or waste material, such as paper, glass, and empty metal cans, so it can be reused.

red blood cell

The most common type of blood cell; it transports oxygen around the body.

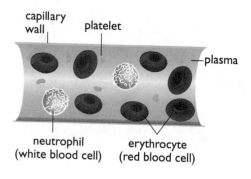

See *blood*.

reflection

The bouncing back of waves when they hit a surface.

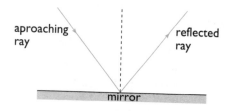

reflex

A very rapid automatic response to a stimulus, for example, the eyes shut when an object suddenly comes near.

refraction

The bending of light when it passes from one substance to another.

renewable energy

Sources of energy that remain in constant supply, for example, solar energy and wind energy. Unlike energy sources such as coal, oil, and natural gas of which there is a limited supply that may eventually be used up.

See *energy*.

repel

To push apart. For example, the poles of two magnets repel each other.

See *magnet, pole*.

reptile

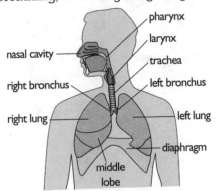

A group of animals with a backbone. Reptiles have a scaly skin and reproduce by means of eggs. Examples include the snake, crocodile, and tortoise. Reptiles are cold-blooded animals.

See *cold-blooded*.

respiratory system

Parts of animal bodies that carry out breathing, including lungs or gills.

Human respiratory system

retina

The part of the eye with sensors that respond to incoming light.

See *eye*.

revolve

To move around a center, such as the movement of the earth around the sun. (This is distinct from the earth rotating on its axis.) The earth takes one year to complete one revolution around the sun.

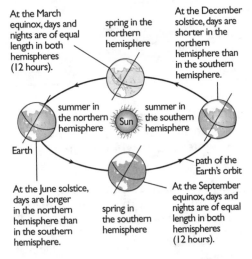

At the March equinox, days and nights are of equal length in both hemispheres (12 hours).

spring in the northern hemisphere

At the December solstice, days are shorter in the northern hemisphere than in the southern hemisphere.

summer in the northern hemisphere

Sun

summer in the southern hemisphere

Earth

path of the Earth's orbit

At the June solstice, days are longer in the northern hemisphere than in the southern hemisphere.

spring in the southern hemisphere

At the September equinox, days and nights are of equal length in both hemispheres (12 hours).

See *rotation*.

rib

One of the bones of the chest that together create a cage around the heart and lungs.

See *skeleton*.

Richter scale

A scale for measuring the strength of earthquakes.

Richter scale	Probable effects
1–3	detectable only by instruments
4	detectable within 32 km of epicenter
5	may cause slight damage
6	moderately destructive
7	a major earthquake
8–9	a very destructive earthquake

See *earthquake.*

rock

In geology, the solid, hard materials that make up the earth's crust. Rocks are composed of one or more minerals.

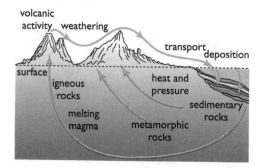

The rock cycle

See *metamorphic rock, mineral, Mohs scale, sedimentary rock, volcanic rock.*

root

The part of plants that anchor them in the soil and act to take up water and minerals.

See *plant.*

rotation

The movement of a body around an axis. Earth rotates on its axis once every 24 hours.

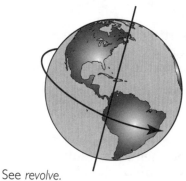

See *revolve.*

Sap moves through tree tissues, up and down from the roots, through the trunk to the leaves, and back.

saliva

Colorless, sticky fluid produced by the salivary glands in the mouth. Important to the digestion of food.

See *mouth.*

salt

One of the chemicals resulting from mixing an acid and a base. Common salt consists of grainy, white crystals obtained from sea water.

See *acid, base.*

sand

Fine fragments of rock consisting of loose grains, often of quartz.

See *quartz.*

sap

Fluid of plants. Sap circulates and carries sugars and minerals that nourish a plant.

satellite

(i) Natural satellite: A body in space that moves around a larger body. The moon is a satellite of Earth.
(ii) Artificial satellite: A device sent into orbit around Earth or another planet. It collects and transmits information to Earth.

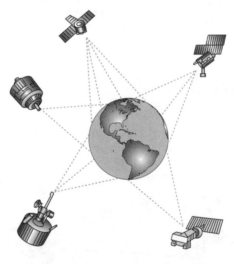

Artificial satellites in orbit around Earth

See *moon.*

Saturn

The sixth planet from the sun.

See *solar system.*

scale

A device used to measure the weight or mass of objects.

scales

Thin, flattened plates that form the covering of fish and reptiles.

scavenger

A term used to describe an animal that eats the flesh of dead animals. The hawk, seagull, hyena, and shark are examples of scavengers.

science

(i) The study of the physical and natural world.
(ii) Knowledge gained of the physical and natural world through experiment and observation.

See *astronomy, bacteriology, biology, botany, chemistry, ecology, entomology, forensic science, genetics, geology, hematology, histology, medicine, meteorology, paleontology, physics, taxonomy, toxicology, veterinary science, zoology.*

science fiction

A story that tells of scientific ideas and settings (especially in some imagined future age). Science fiction may be about space or time travel or life on other planets. Examples of science fiction are the *Star Wars* movies and the book *The Time Machine* by H. G. Wells.

scientific method

A process of gaining knowledge by experimenting and observing.

See *demonstrate, discover, estimate, experiment, hypothesis, identify, investigate, observe, test, theory.*

scientific name

A name given to each species of living things. A scientific name consists of the genus name and the species name. For example, the genus name "Panthera" is used to name various cat species: *Panthera leo* (the lion), *Panthera tigris* (the tiger), *Panthera onca* (the jaguar) and *Panthera pardus* (the leopard).

Scientific name	Panthera leo
Genus	Panthera
Species	leo
Common name	lion

See *classification.*

scorpion

An arachnid that has a long, narrow tail with a sting at the end. Closely related to the spider.

See *arachnid, spider.*

See *starfish.*

screw

A thin metal cylinder or cone with a spiral thread on the outside or inside. Used in joining a range of materials, for example, wood, metal, and plastics.

See *machine.*

seaweed

One of the algae plants that grow in the sea.

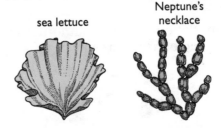

sea lettuce

Neptune's necklace

Examples of seaweed

season

Time of the year marked by particular conditions of weather or temperature.

	Northern Hemisphere	Southern Hemisphere
June–August	summer	winter
September–November	autumn	spring
December–January	winter	summer
March–May	spring	autumn

sedimentary rock

A type of rock made up of layers of small pieces of eroded rock. This type of rock is pressed in layers and cemented over many years. Layers are often visible in the rocks. Examples of sedimentary rock include sandstone and limestone.

seastar

See *starfish.*

sea urchin

A sea creature with a globe-shaped body covered with small plates. Member of the echinoderm (spiny skinned) group. The spines project from the surface.

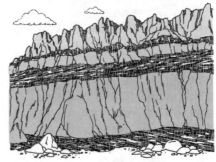

Sedimentary rock layers

See *rock.*

seed

Produced by a plant with flowers or cones. A new plant grows from the seed. Method of reproduction.

See *germ, germinate*.

sense

One of the abilities that enable us to see, touch, hear, taste, or smell.

See *ear, eye, hearing, nose, sight, taste, tongue*.

shadow

Shade created by something blocking a light source, for example, a body's shadow on a wall occurs because the body prevents the light from shining on the wall.

shark

A sea fish with a skeleton of cartilage. Examples include the Great White shark, hammerhead, sand shark, and lemon shark.

See *cartilage, fish*.

shooting star

A faint glow in the sky from a meteor.

See *meteor*.

sight

The sensing of light.

See *eye, sense*.

silt

Very fine deposits of grainy material left behind or deposited by running water. A flowing river may deposit silt when it reaches a lake.

siphon

A tube through which water moves from one container to another.

skeleton

Bones of an animal that fit together to make its framework. For vertebrates, such as humans, the skeleton is inside the body. For invertebrates, such as the lobster, the skeleton is outside the body.

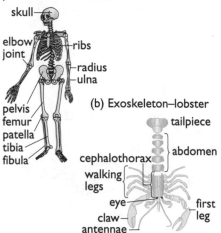

(a) Endoskeleton–human
skull
elbow joint
ribs
radius
ulna
pelvis
femur
patella
tibia
fibula

(b) Exoskeleton–lobster
tailpiece
abdomen
cephalothorax
walking legs
eye
claw
antennae
first leg

See *femur, fibula, hip, knee, radius, rib, skull, tibia, ulna*.

skin

The soft outer covering of an animal's body.

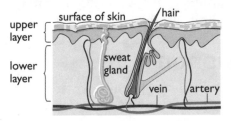

See *fur.*

skull

The bony covering of the head that protects the brain and sense organs.

See *skeleton.*

slate

Igneous rock consisting mostly of quartz and mica. True slate is hard and compact. Slate is used as roofing material and for paving stones and flooring. Slate is commonly bluish-black or grey in color.

See *igneous rock, rock.*

slater

A wood louse. Greyish crustacean with shelled body of segments and many legs. Some slaters are able to roll into a ball.

See *crustacean.*

slope

To slant or tilt upward or downward.

See *gradient, incline.*

slug

A type of soft-bodied, slimy mollusk without a shell (unlike a snail, which has a shell). Slugs inhabit damp places.

See *invertebrate, mollusk.*

small intestine

A narrow tube in an animal's body that connects the stomach to the large intestine. Digested food is absorbed into the bloodstream here.

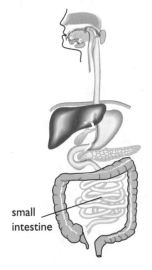

Human digestive system

See *digestive system, intestine.*

smell

The sensing of odor or scent.

See *nose.*

smog

Cloud of smoke and fog.
See *fog.*

snail

A type of soft-bodied, slimy mollusk with a shell. The land species inhabit damp places. Marine species, for example, the black elephant snail and the periwinkle, inhabit warm shallow waters as well as ocean floors.

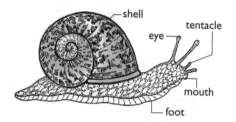

Land snail

See *invertebrate, mollusk, slug.*

snake

A legless reptile with dry scaly skin and a forked tongue. Examples include the boa constrictor, rattlesnake, and tiger snake.
See *reptile.*

snow

Frozen raindrops that fall as transparent ice crystals or flakes.

sodium

Soft, silvery white metal. Found in salt, bicarbonate of soda, and lye.
See *metal, salt.*

software

A collection of programs that run on a computer.

soil

A loose layer of materials of the earth's surface. Soil consists of broken-down rock, humus, water, gases, and minerals. Plants tend to grow best in topsoil.

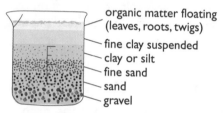

Soil shaken with water and allowed to settle

solar eclipse

When the moon passes between the sun and the earth. A shadow is cast on part of the earth's surface.

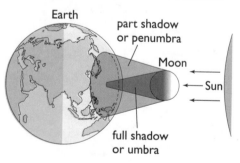

Solar eclipse

See *eclipse.*

solar energy

Energy produced by the sun. Solar energy can be captured in solar cells for use as an energy source.

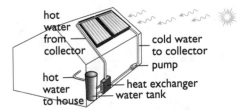

Sunlight heats solar collectors on the top of the roof to supply hot water.

See *renewable energy.*

solar system

Our sun, together with the nine planets, their satellites (moons), the asteroids, comets, and meteorites that revolve around it.

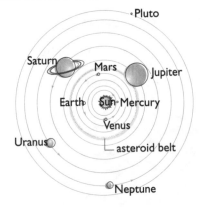

See *planet, sun.*

solid

One of the states of matter (solid, liquid, gas). Material that has shape and form of its own. Three-dimensional.

See *matter.*

solubility

The ease with which a substance dissolves in another substance. Salt is very soluble in water, but sand is not soluble at all. Most substances are more soluble in hot liquids than in cold. Gases are different. Carbon dioxide gas, for example, dissolves better in cold water than in warm water.

sound

A form of energy produced by vibration and sensed by the ear.

See *acoustics, ear, hearing, wave.*

species

A group of organisms that resemble each other. Members of each group breed with others in the group to produce offspring.

See *scientific name, taxonomy.*

spectrum

A band of colors seen when white light is passed through a prism.

See *prism.*

speed

The rate at which an object travels over a distance. Speed is measured by dividing distance traveled by the time it takes. An automobile that travels 25 miles in 30 minutes is moving at an average speed of 25 miles per half hour or 50 miles per hour.

sperm

A tadpole-shaped single cell that carries the hereditary traits of a male parent. When a sperm enters an egg—a process called fertilization—the egg begins to divide to produce a new individual with characteristics from both the male and female parents.

See *egg, fertilize.*

spider

An invertebrate animal with eight jointed legs and two body parts. Member of the arachnid group of animals. Most spiders produce silk at their spinnerets.

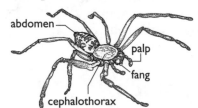

abdomen

palp

fang

cephalothorax

See *arachnid, scorpion.*

sponge

A simple water animal that lives attached to rocks. A sponge feeds on plankton by drawing water through pores in its body. Sponge skeletons are used by humans for washing.

spore

A microscopic particle, produced by simple plants, that develops into an adult without being fertilized. Moss, fern, fungi, and bacteria grow from a spore.

See *fern, moss.*

spring

(i)   The season between winter and summer; March, April, and May in the Northern Hemisphere; September, October, and November in the Southern Hemisphere.

See *season.*

(ii)   An object with the ability to fly back, recoil, or move rapidly, for example, springs in a mattress.

(iii) A place where water or oil comes to the surface from under the ground.

stalactite

Hanging columns of calcium carbonate. Stalactite form from the ceiling or wall of a cave by evaporation of dripping water.

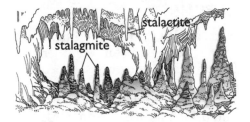

stalactite

stalagmite

See *stalagmite.*

stalagmite

A column of calcium carbonate that forms from the floor of a cave by dripping water.

See *stalactite*.

star

One of millions of large gaseous bodies in space. A star gives off its own light. The sun is a star.

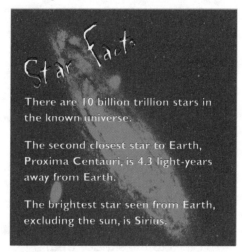

Star Facts

There are 10 billion trillion stars in the known universe.

The second closest star to Earth, Proxima Centauri, is 4.3 light-years away from Earth.

The brightest star seen from Earth, excluding the sun, is Sirius.

starch

Food storage material of plants; carbohydrate occurring in potatoes, wheat, rice, and oats.

See *carbohydrate*.

starfish

A sea creature without a backbone, in the shape of a star. Member of the echinoderm (spiny skinned) group. Its arms contain many tubed feet that it uses to move and attach itself to its prey. Also known as a seastar.

static electricity

Electricity not moving as a current. Lightning is an example of static electricity.

See *lightning*.

steam

Gaseous vapor produced by boiling water. Used to power steam engines.

See *condensation, vapor.*

steel

A strong, hard metal that is a mixture of iron and carbon or other elements. Steel is very strong and is nonreactive. Used to make tools.

See *metal.*

stem

The stalk of a plant that usually grows upward from the root.

See *anatomy, plant.*

stethoscope

An instrument used to listen to the sounds made by the heart and lungs.

stomach

A baglike organ that is part of the digestive system; between the esophagus and small intestine. The stomach produces digestive liquids. Stomach muscles squeeze and mix food with liquids.

See *digestive system, small intestine.*

succession

The process by which one community of plants and animals replaces another over time.
See *community*.

suction

A force caused by pressure differences. The action of sucking can remove air. A vacuum cleaner removes dirt particles through suction.

sugar

A sweet crystalline substance. Sugar is obtained from beets and sugar cane. Member of the carbohydrate class of foods.
See *carbohydrate*.

sun

The central star of our solar system. Planets and other bodies revolve around the sun. The sun radiates heat and light.

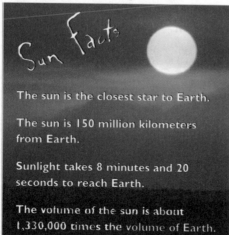

Sun Facts

The sun is the closest star to Earth.

The sun is 150 million kilometers from Earth.

Sunlight takes 8 minutes and 20 seconds to reach Earth.

The volume of the sun is about 1,330,000 times the volume of Earth.

See *solar system, star*.

sundial

A device that uses sunlight to tell the time during the day. A shadow is cast on the face of the sundial, which is marked in hours.

swallow

To pass food and saliva down the esophagus, using the tongue, the throat, and neck muscles.

switch

A device that is part of an electronic or electric circuit and controls the flow of electric current.

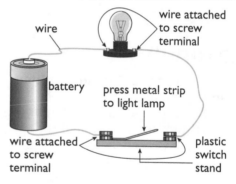

wire

wire attached to screw terminal

battery

press metal strip to light lamp

wire attached to screw terminal

plastic switch stand

Simple electric circuit and switch

synthetic

A material that is artificial or made by humans. Synthetic materials include plastics, nylon, polyester, and vinyl.

tadpole

A young frog or toad after hatching, before it is a fully developed adult.

See *amphibian, frog, metamorphosis.*

taste

Experiencing the flavor of foods sensed by the tongue.

See *sense, tongue.*

taxonomy

Another name for the classification of living things. The science of classifying; the system of assigning living things to groups, giving each one a species name.

See *classification, scientific name.*

technology

The study and application of techniques, systems, and skills, especially of the sciences applied to industry. Ranging from simple to the most complex.

teflon

Synthetic material that is very heat resistant and does not react readily. Used for many purposes, including nonstick cookware.

See *synthetic.*

telephone

An instrument used for talking to someone at a distance. It works by converting sound to electrical signals and back again.

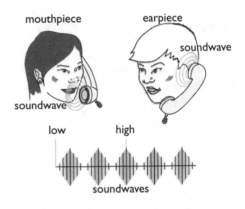

telescope

A device with lenses and mirrors for viewing things at a distance. Used to make distant objects look nearer and larger.

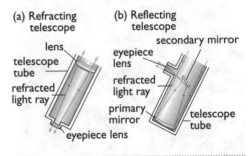

television

A device for receiving picture and sound signals. An image is projected on a picture tube for viewing.

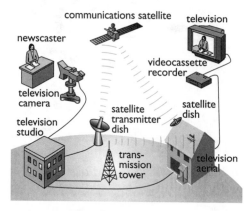

temperature

A measure of how hot or cold something is. Temperature is measured using a thermometer.

See *thermometer.*

tendon

A strand or sheet of material connecting muscle to bone. Thin cords of connective tissue.

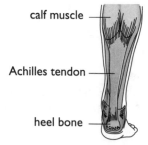

The leg and foot. The Achilles tendon runs from the calf muscle down to the heel bone.

See *bone, muscle.*

tentacle

A long, thin extension of soft-bodied animals, used for feeling, grasping, or moving. An octopus, slug, and snail use tentacles in this way.

See *mollusk, octopus, snail.*

terrestrial

Anything that relates to Earth. The rocky inner planets of the solar system, Mercury, Venus, and Mars, are called terrestrial planets because they consist of material similar to that of Earth.

See *solar system.*

test

A trial or experiment to check a prediction, as in "Let's conduct a test to find which material is the lightest."

See *theory.*

theory

A set of ideas used to explain a range of connected observations. A theory is a hypothesis that has been supported by many experiments. Examples include the theory of evolution and the theory of plate tectonics.

thermal

Relating to temperature. Thermal air currents are caused by temperature differences in the atmosphere.

See *temperature.*

thermometer

A device for measuring how hot or cold something is using the Celsius scale or the Fahrenheit scale. There are many types designed to measure temperatures of different objects.

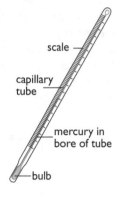

scale

capillary tube

mercury in bore of tube

bulb

thorax

(i)   In animals with backbones, the part of the body containing the lungs and heart.
(ii) In insects, the thorax carries the wings and legs.
(iii) In spiders and crustaceans, the thorax is fused with the head into a cephalothorax.

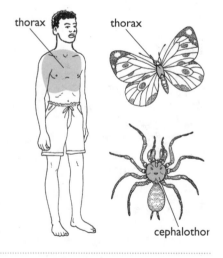

thorax

thorax

cephalothor

thrust

A forward push, as in the force pushing a plane through propellers, or the lift of a rocket.

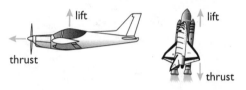

lift

thrust

lift

thrust

See *drag, gravity, lift*.

thunder

A low, rumbling sound associated with lightning.

See *lightning*.

tibia

The larger of the two lower leg bones; shin bones.

See *skeleton*.

tide

The regular rise and fall of sea level, occurring approximately twice a day. Caused by the pull of the moon, and also the sun, on the earth.

time

The passage of existence divided into intervals, measured in years, days, hours, minutes, and seconds.

toad

An animal in the same group as frogs. It has dry skin and spends most of its time on land. An amphibian.

See *amphibian*.

toadstool

Umbrella-shaped fungus. Some are edible, and others are poisonous.

See *fungus*.

tongue

A muscular organ in the mouth. It is used for tasting, licking, and to help with eating and swallowing. In humans, also used for talking.

tool

An instrument or device used to do a job. A hammer, saw, axe, wrench, spade, carving knife, and garlic press are examples of common tools.

tooth

A hard bonelike structure in the mouth used for chewing and biting. Humans have two sets of teeth. There are 20 first teeth (called deciduous or milk teeth), which are replaced after age 6 by 32 permanent teeth.

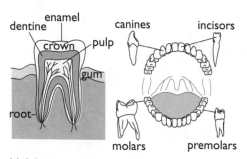

(a) A human tooth   (b) A set of adult teeth

topsoil

The top layer of soil, seen when digging down through the surface of the earth. The topsoil layer is often darker, containing humus, the remains of plant and animal material.

See *soil*.

tornado

A violently rotating column of air that sometimes reaches downward from a thunder storm and usually appears as a funnel-shaped cloud. Wind speed in a tornado can exceed 300 miles per hour. Oklahoma City has been struck by more than 100 tornadoes, more than any other city in the United States.

tortoise

A vertebrate from the group called reptiles; has a hard protective shell and usually lives on land.

See *reptile, turtle*.

touch

The sensing of pressure, temperature, and pain in the skin.

See *sense, skin.*

toxic

Referring to a substance that can be a hazard to living things; poisonous.

See *hazard label.*

toxic

toxicology

A branch of medicine dealing with poisons.

See *toxic.*

transmit

To send, for example, to transmit a television or radio signal.

See *television.*

transparent

Describing material through which light can travel, for example, glass or clear plastic. One can see through a window because the glass is transparent.

transpire

To lose water due to evaporation, as occurs through the leaves of plants.

See *evaporation, leaf.*

tree

A long-lived, upright plant with a large woody main stem or trunk. Examples are the oak, spruce, aspen, pine, birch, maple, and elm.

turtle

A vertebrate from the group called reptiles; has a hard protective shell and lives in the water.

See *reptile, tortoise.*

ulcer

One of a variety of sores that can occur on the surface of the skin or on the inside linings of the body, for example, a stomach ulcer.

ulna

One of the two bones of the forearm of vertebrates.

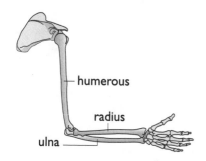

humerous

radius

ulna

The human arm

See *skeleton.*

ultrasound

Very high frequency sound waves that the human ear is unable to hear. Animals that can hear higher frequencies, such as bats and porpoises, make use of ultrasound to detect objects, for example, when hunting for food. Ultrasound is widely used in medical diagnosis.

ultraviolet ray

Light that has a shorter wavelength than visible light. The human eye cannot detect it. It occurs as part of sunlight. The sun is a powerful source of ultraviolet rays. Overexposure to the sun's ultraviolet rays produces sunburn.

See *electromagnetic spectrum.*

umbilical cord

A tube that connects the unborn baby to its mother's body in placental mammals. Food is carried to the baby and wastes are taken away in this tube. It is cut at birth, and the stump left on the baby shrivels to form the navel.

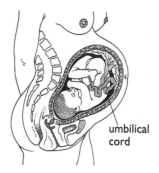

umbilical cord

Human fetus

universe

All of space and all galaxies that exist in it.

See *galaxy, Milky Way.*

uranium

White, radioactive, naturally occurring substance. Used to produce energy and nuclear weapons.

See *radioactive*.

Uranus

The seventh planet from the sun.

See *solar system*.

urchin

See *sea urchin*.

urethra

Urine leaves the bladder through the urethra, a tube that leads out of the body.

See *excretory system, urine*.

urine

Liquid produced by the kidneys when they remove waste from the blood. Stored in the bladder and passed from the body through the urethra.

See *excretory system*.

vaccine

A changed form of a virus injected to produce antibodies and build up resistance to disease caused by that virus.

vacuum

Space with no matter in it. A complete or total vacuum cannot exist. A container with pressure much lower than the outside pressure is called a vacuum.

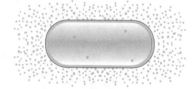

vacuum flask

A container for keeping things hot or cold, designed to reduce heat transfer.

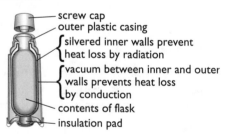

screw cap
outer plastic casing
{ silvered inner walls prevent heat loss by radiation
{ vacuum between inner and outer walls prevents heat loss by conduction
contents of flask
insulation pad

valve

(i) In general, a device to control the flow of a liquid or gas.
(ii) An electron tube; a glass tube at low pressure used to control the flow of electricity in a circuit.
(iii) In animals, a structure to control the direction of the flow of blood.

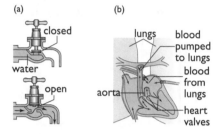

(a) closed
water
open

(b) lungs blood pumped to lungs
blood from lungs
aorta
heart valves

(a) The valve in a tap controls water flow.
(b) The valve in the heart controls blood flow.

vapor

Gas that can turn to a liquid.

See *condensation, gas.*

variable

A quantity (independent variable) that is being manipulated in an experiment in order to test its effect on another quantity (dependent variable). In an experiment to test the absorbency of different brands of paper towels, the brands being tested are the independent variable and the amount of water is the dependent variable.

See *experiment.*

vegetable

Any of a number of different plants whose roots, fruit, leaves, stems, or seeds are used for food, for example, cabbage, potato, lettuce, onion, and celery.

vegetation

The plant growth of a certain area.

vein

A blood vessel through which blood flows back to the heart.

See *artery*.

venom

The poison secreted by some animals such as snakes and spiders.

ventricle

A chamber or cavity. Especially used to describe certain chambers of the heart and brain.

See *heart*.

Venus

The second planet from the sun.

See *solar system*.

vertebra

One of the bones of the backbone or spine. The spine is made up of 33 vertebrae.

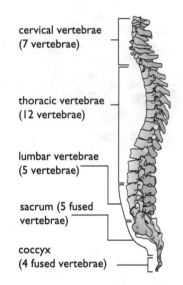

cervical vertebrae (7 vertebrae)

thoracic vertebrae (12 vertebrae)

lumbar vertebrae (5 vertebrae)

sacrum (5 fused vertebrae)

coccyx (4 fused vertebrae)

vertebrate

An animal with a backbone.

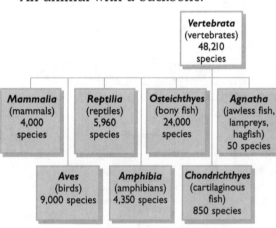

veterinary science

The study of diseases in animals in order to prevent and cure them.

vibrate

To move rapidly back and forth or up and down, as seen in a string of a guitar or on the surface of a drum.

See *wave*.

vinegar

A liquid containing acetic acid; tastes sour. Used to pickle food; can be made from wine.

vinyl

A tough plastic synthetic material with a range of uses including furniture coverings and clothing.
See *synthetic.*

virus

(i) A living thing smaller than bacteria, capable of living and growing only inside a host cell. Viruses are the only living things not made up of cells. Viruses are the cause of many diseases, including the common cold, influenza (flu), AIDS, and many plant diseases.

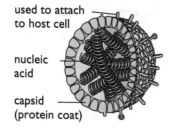

used to attach to host cell

nucleic acid

capsid (protein coat)

The structure of a virus

(ii) In computing, a piece of software that can copy itself.

viscous

Describing the thickness of a liquid. Liquids such as honey and mud are very viscous and therefore resist flowing. Water is low in viscosity and flows easily.
See *liquid.*

visible light

The range of the spectrum of electromagnetic waves to which the human eye responds.
See *electromagnetic spectrum, eye, light.*

vitamin

A chemical necessary in small amounts for the healthy functioning of the body.

Vitamin	Main function	Deficiency disease
B_1	regulation of carbohydrate metabolism	beriberi
B_2	converts food to energy	range of symptoms
B_6	metabolism of amino acids	nervous system & skin disorders
B_{12}	for cell metabolism, particularly nerve cells	pernicious anemia
A	structure of skin and mucus-secreting tissue	blindness, infection
C	structure of connective tissue, absorption of iron	scurvy
D	transport of calcium from blood to bone	rickets
E	protects essential fatty acids from free radicals	range of symptoms

voice

The sound produced by vibrations in the vocal chords located in the throat.

volcanic rock

Rock formed by the activity of volcanoes. Also called igneous rock. There are two main types.

(i) Rocks formed from lava flowing out of a volcano, called lava rocks.

(ii) Rocks formed by being blown out of the volcano, called pyroclastic rocks.

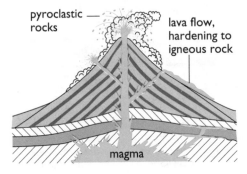

See *volcano*.

volcano

A crack in the earth's crust; typically, a cone-shaped hill having a central crater with a pipe leading to magma below. The center of a volcanic eruption.

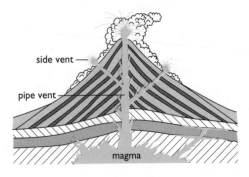

volt

The unit of electrical force, which can be measured with a voltmeter.

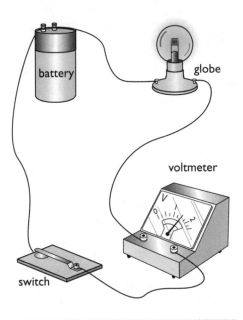

voltage

The force that pushes each electron around an electric circuit; commonly used term for the correct term "potential difference."

See *volt*.

volume

(i) The loudness of sound.

See *sound*.

(ii) A measure of capacity.

warm-blooded

A term used to describe creatures with body temperatures that remain the same despite changes in the surrounding temperature. Mammals and birds are warm-blooded animals. The normal body temperature of humans is 37°C or 98.6°F.

See *Celsius scale, cold-blooded, Fahrenheit scale.*

wasp

A four-winged insect with a sting at the tail end. Closely related to a bee.

See *insect.*

waste

(i) Rubbish, litter, scraps, unwanted substances.
(ii) Material passing out of the body.

See *feces, urine.*

water

Clear, colorless and odorless liquid; a form of water, such as rain.

See *liquid.*

water cycle

The circulation of water on Earth and in Earth's atmosphere.

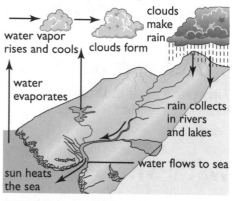

water energy

Movement energy produced by flowing water.

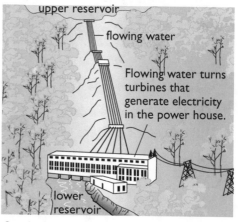

See *hydroelectric energy.*

water erosion

The carrying away of rock and soil by water. For example, when waves pound the shore they carry away soil and rock and so change the shoreline.

See *erosion.*

water pressure

A force produced by water. For example, opening a tap forces the water out because of the pressure built up in the water pipe.

water vapor

Tiny particles of moisture suspended in air. Steam, mist.

See *gas, vapor.*

waterwheel

A wheel that is rotated by flowing water. Used to drive machinery or raise water for irrigation.

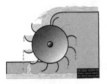

See *water energy.*

watt

A unit of electric power.

A 100-watt light bulb is brighter than a 40-watt light bulb.

See *electricity.*

wave

The transfer of energy from one place to another, as in water, earthquake, light, sound, and microwave.

(a) Water waves

(b) Earthquake waves

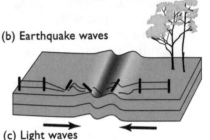

(c) Light waves

(d) Microwaves

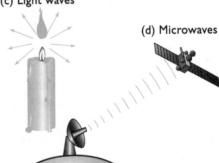

See *electromagnetic spectrum, light, motion, sound, vibrate.*

wavelength

The distance from the crest of one wave to the crest of the next. Period of one complete wave.

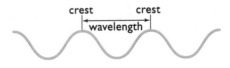

See *wave.*

weather

Conditions and movement of the atmosphere at any one place or time. Aspects of weather include heat and cold, amount of sunshine, cloudiness, humidity, rain, snow, fog, and wind strength and direction.

See *weather forecasting.*

weather forecasting

Predicting weather using devices located on land, water, and high above the earth to scan the weather.

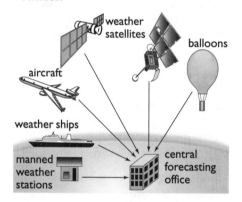

weathering

The wearing away of soil or rocks into small bits by wind, water, ice, or frequent disturbance of the ground by animals or people.

See *erosion.*

weather station

Weather is measured at a series of weather stations located around the globe. Weather stations use equipment to gather information on weather.

See *weather, weather forecasting.*

wedge

A simple machine that consists of two inclined planes joined together. It is used to split things or force things apart.

See *machine.*

weed

A plant that is of no use to people or animals.

See *plant.*

weight

The gravitational pull of an object. The weight of an object changes with the change of the gravitational pull. The mass of an object remains the same in different gravities.

See *gravity, mass.*

weightlessness

A condition of having little or no weight. Free from pull of gravity. Astronauts in space experience weightlessness. They cannot keep their feet on the floor since there is no gravity to hold their weight down.

See *gravity.*

whale

The largest living mammal. A sea mammal of which there are many species, for example, the blue whale, southern right whale, and sperm whale. The blue whale is the largest animal that has ever lived; often weighs 100 tons.

See *mammal.*

wheel

A simple machine that consists of a circular frame or disk. It turns on an axle.

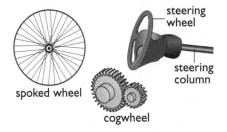

Some types of wheels

See *axle, gear, machine, waterwheel.*

white blood cell

The cell of the blood that helps to protect the body against disease. Scientifically known as a leucocyte.

See *blood, disease.*

wind

Moving air.
See *Beaufort wind scale, wind vane.*

wind vane

An instrument that turns when blown by the wind. It shows the direction in which the wind is blowing. Wind is named by the direction from which it blows. For example, a northeasterly is blowing from the northeast.

wool

Soft, greasy hair that grows on sheep and other animals. Wool is shorn from the animal and spun to make thread. Woolen thread is woven or knitted to make articles of clothing.

work

Effort used to move an object. In the study of physics, work is calculated by multiplying the mass by the distance moved.

The same amount of work is done in each case.

worm

A long, slender, soft-bodied invertebrate. Examples include the earthworm, flatworm, tapeworm, and segmented worm.

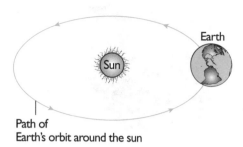

Path of
Earth's orbit around the sun

See *revolve.*

X-ray

(i) Radiation of particular wavelengths in the electromagnetic spectrum.

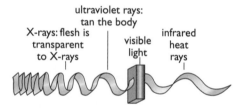

ultraviolet rays:
tan the body
X-rays: flesh is
transparent
to X-rays

visible
light

infrared
heat
rays

(ii) An image produced as a photograph when X-rays are directed through an object.

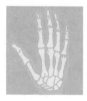

year

The period of time it takes the earth to make one complete revolution around the sun.

yeast

A type of fungus. It feeds on sugar and starch. As it feeds it gives off carbon dioxide gas. Carbon dioxide makes bread dough rise before baking.

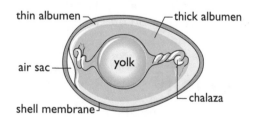

balls of fresh
yeast dough

Action of yeast, water, sugar, and flour expands dough.

yolk

Food stored in an egg. In a fertile egg, the yolk provides food for a growing embryo (early stage of life).

thin albumen

thick albumen

air sac

yolk

shell membrane

chalaza

See *albumen.*

zenith

The highest point in the sky. The area directly above the head of a person observing the sky.

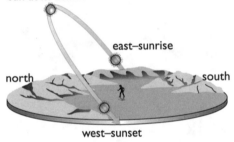

sun at its zenith

east–sunrise

north

south

west–sunset

zinc

A hard, white metal. Zinc is used in electric batteries and as a protective coating on steel.

See *metal.*

zoology

The study of members of the animal kingdom.

zoo plankton

Small, drifting animals found in watery environments.

See *plankton.*

zygote

The name given to an egg cell after it has been fertilized.

See *fertilize.*

Appendices

Appendix I   Living things

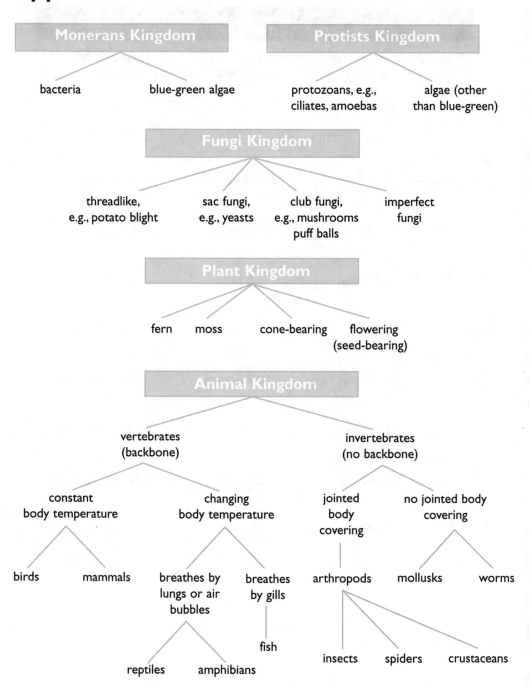

Appendix II

Planets in the solar system

Planet	Length of diameter	Length of one rotation (day and night)	Length of one year
Mercury	4,900 km	59 days	88 days
Venus	12,100 km	243 days	224.7 days
Earth	12,756 km	24 hours	365.3 days
Mars	6,800 km	24.5 hours	687 days
Jupiter	142,800 km	9.8 hours	12 Earth years
Saturn	120,660 km	10.7 hours	29.5 Earth years
Uranus	51,500 km	17 hours	84 Earth years
Neptune	49,500 km	16 hours	165 Earth years
Pluto	2,300 km	6 days	248 Earth years

Our Planet Chart

Distance from the sun	Number of moons	Number of rings
57.9 million km	None	None
108.2 million km	None	None
149.6 million km	1	None
227.8 million km	2	None
778 million km	At least 16	2
1,427 million km	At least 17	Many
2,870 million km	At least 15	10
4,500 million km	8	4
5,900 million km	1	None

Appendix III
Geological time scale

Era	Period	Meaning of period name
Precambrian (meaning before Cambrian period)	Archean	Ancient or primitive
	Proterozoic	Time of earliest life
Paleozoic (meaning ancient life)	Cambrian	From Latin word meaning "water"
	Ordovician	Named after an ancient Welsh tribe Rocks of this period were first studied in Wales.
	Silurian	Named after an ancient British tribe in area where these rocks were first studied
	Devonian	Named after Devonshire in Britain where these rocks were first studied
	Carboniferous	Containing carbon as in coal deposits
	Permian	Named after an area in Russia called Perm
Mesozoic (meaning middle life)	Triassic	First of three periods of middle life
	Jurassic	Named after the Jura mountains in France where the rocks were first studied
	Cretaceous	From Latin word meaning "chalk"
Cenozoic or Caenozoic (meaning recent life)	Tertiary	Third period The period following the Mesozoic
	Quaternary	Fourth period

Major Events	Age in mya (millions of years ago)
No life exists on Earth.	3,600–2,500
Life develops.	2,500–570
Earliest fossil forms develop.	570–500
Animal life in seas includes reef-building algae and jawless fishes.	500–435
Large reefs formed by coral-like life. First jawed fishes evolve. Plants begin to invade the land.	435–410
Amphibians and insects develop.	410–360
Large plants, such as tree ferns, are abundant.	360–290
Cone-bearing trees develop.	290–235
World climate is dry. Early dinosaurs and reptiles exist. Mammals evolve.	235–195
Climate wetter, giving rise to large forests. Dinosaurs are abundant. Birds evolve.	195–135
Flowering (seed-bearing) plants evolve. Dinosaurs flourish and die out at the end of the period.	135–65
Mammals flourish.	65–2
Human species evolves.	2–present

Appendix IV

Some scientists and inventors

Name	Dates	Field
Aristotle	384–322 B.C.	Science Logic
Beaufort, Sir Francis	1774–1857	Hydrography
Curie, Marie	1867–1933	Physics Chemistry
Darwin, Charles	1809–1882	Nature
Edison, Thomas	1847–1931	Inventions
Einstein, Albert	1879–1955	Physics
Galilei, Galileo	1564–1642	Astronomy Physics
Halley, Edmond	1656–1742	Astronomy
Herschel, Caroline	1750–1848	Astronomy
Hubble, Edwin	1889–1953	Astronomy
Levi-Montalcini, Rita	1909–	Medical Science
Lovelace, Ada Byron	1815–1852	Mathematics
McClintock, Barbara	1902–1992	Genetics
Mohs, Friedrich	1775–1858	Mineralogy
Newton, Isaac	1642–1727	Physics Astronomy Mathematics
Pasteur, Louis	1822–1895	Chemistry
Richter, Charles F.	1900–1985	Seismology

Achievements

Described as one of the greatest thinkers. Believed in careful observation and detailed classification

Devised the Beaufort scale, which describes the force of winds

Researched radiation and shared Nobel Prize in Physics
Discovered radium and awarded Nobel Prize in Chemistry

Developed the theory of natural selection and evolution

Invented the phonograph. Manufactured the first light bulbs

Created the Special Theory of Relativity and the General Theory of Relativity

Discovered the laws governing falling bodies
Discovered the lunar valleys and mountains of the moon's surface

Calculated the orbit of a comet and demonstrated that a comet moves in an elliptical orbit around the sun

Discovered at least five comets, several nebulae, and star clusters

Proved the existence of galaxies other than our own

Researched cell and organ growth
Shared Nobel Prize for Medicine and Physiology

Devised a computer program and developed the idea of punched cards

Discovered that genes can change their positions on chromosomes (which is important for the understanding of hereditary processes)
Awarded Nobel Prize for Medicine 1983

Devised the scale of hardness of minerals

Demonstrated that the planets were pulled around the sun by gravitation
Demonstrated that sunlight consists of a mixture of colors

Founded the science of bacteriology
Discovered that diseases are spread by bacteria

Developed the Richter scale, which measures the ground motion caused by an earthquake

My own Science and Technology words: